Java™ 6 Platform Revealed

John Zukowski

Apress®

Java™ 6 Platform Revealed

Copyright © 2006 by John Zukowski

ISBN-13 (pbk): 978-1-59059-660-9

ISBN-10 (pbk): 1-59059-660-9

Printed and bound in the United States of America 9 8 7 6 5 4 3 2 1

Trademarked names may appear in this book. Rather than use a trademark symbol with every occurrence of a trademarked name, we use the names only in an editorial fashion and to the benefit of the trademark owner, with no intention of infringement of the trademark.

Java and all Java-based marks are trademarks or registered trademarks of Sun Microsystems, Inc., in the US and other countries.

Apress, Inc. is not affiliated with Sun Microsystems, Inc., and this book was written without endorsement from Sun Microsystems, Inc.

Lead Editor: Steve Anglin
Technical Reviewer: Sumit Pal
Editorial Board: Steve Anglin, Ewan Buckingham, Gary Cornell, Jason Gilmore, Jonathan Gennick,
    Jonathan Hassell, James Huddleston, Chris Mills, Matthew Moodie, Dominic Shakeshaft,
    Jim Sumser, Keir Thomas, Matt Wade
Project Manager: Kylie Johnston
Copy Edit Manager: Nicole LeClerc
Copy Editor: Damon Larson
Assistant Production Director: Kari Brooks-Copony
Production Editor: Laura Esterman
Compositor: Dina Quan
Proofreader: Elizabeth Berry
Indexer: Toma Mulligan
Cover Designer: Kurt Krames
Manufacturing Director: Tom Debolski

Distributed to the book trade worldwide by Springer-Verlag New York, Inc., 233 Spring Street, 6th Floor, New York, NY 10013. Phone 1-800-SPRINGER, fax 201-348-4505, e-mail orders-ny@springer-sbm.com, or visit http://www.springeronline.com.

For information on translations, please contact Apress directly at 2560 Ninth Street, Suite 219, Berkeley, CA 94710. Phone 510-549-5930, fax 510-549-5939, e-mail info@apress.com, or visit http://www.apress.com.

The information in this book is distributed on an "as is" basis, without warranty. Although every precaution has been taken in the preparation of this work, neither the author(s) nor Apress shall have any liability to any person or entity with respect to any loss or damage caused or alleged to be caused directly or indirectly by the information contained in this work.

The source code for this book is available to readers at http://www.apress.com in the Source Code section.

Contents at a Glance

Contents

About the Author

JOHN ZUKOWSKI has been involved with the Java platform since it was just called Java, 11 years and running, since 1995. He is actively working with SavaJe Technologies to finish up the JavaOne 2006 device of show: the Jasper S20 mobile phone. He currently writes a monthly column for Sun's Core Java Technologies Tech Tips (http://java.sun.com/developer/JDCTechTips) and Technology Fundamentals Newsletter (http://java.sun.com/developer/onlineTraining/new2java/supplements). He has contributed content to numerous other sites, including jGuru (www.jguru.com), DevX (www.devx.com), Intel (www.intel.com), and JavaWorld (www.javaworld.com). He has written many other popular titles on Java, including *Java AWT Reference* (O'Reilly), *Mastering Java 2* (Sybex), *Borland's JBuilder: No Experience Required* (Sybex), *Learn Java with JBuilder 6* (Apress), *Java Collections* (Apress), and *The Definitive Guide to Java Swing* (Apress).

About the Technical Reviewer

 **SUMIT PAL** has about 12 years of experience with software architecture, design, and development on a variety of platforms, including J2EE. Sumit worked with the SQL Server replication group while with Microsoft for 2 years, and with Oracle's OLAP Server group while with Oracle for 7 years.

In addition to certifications including IEEE CSDP and J2EE Architect, Sumit has an MS in computer science from the Asian Institute of Technology, Thailand.

Sumit has keen interest in database internals, algorithms, and search engine technology.

Sumit has invented some basic generalized algorithms to find divisibility between numbers, and has also invented divisibility rules for prime numbers less than 100.

Currently, he loves to play as much as he can with his 22-month-old daughter.

Acknowledgments

Who knew how long my tenth book would take to do? It is always fun to write about a moving target—the API set has been evolving as I've written each chapter, and even after I turned them in. Now that we're done, thanks need to go out to a whole bunch of people.

For starters, there is everyone at Apress. Some days I wonder how they've put up with me for so long. To my project manager, Kylie Johnston, and my editor, Steve Anglin: thanks, we finally made it to the end. For Damon Larson, it was great working with you. Other than that one chapter I wanted back after submitting, hopefully this was one of your easier editing jobs. For Laura Esterman and everyone working with the page proofs: this was much easier than it was with my second book, when we had to snail-mail PDFs back and forth. To my tech reviewer, Sumit Pal: thanks for all the input and requests for more details to get things described just right, as well as those rapid turnarounds to keep things on schedule due to my delays.

A book on Mustang can't go without thanking all the folks making it happen, especially Mark Reinhold, the spec lead for JSR 270. It was nice getting all those little tidbits on how to use the latest feature of the week in everyone's blogs. The timing on some of them couldn't have been better.

For the readers, thanks for all the comments about past books. It's always nice to hear how something I wrote helped you solve a problem more quickly. Hopefully, the tradition continues with this book.

As always, there are the random folks I'd like to thank for things that happened since the last book. To Dan Jacobs, a good friend and great co-worker: best of luck with your latest endeavors. Mary Maguire, thanks for the laugh at JavaOne when you took out the "Sold Out" sign. Of course, we needed it later that same first day. Venkat Kanthimathinath, thanks for giving me a tour around Chennai when I was in town. My appreciation of the country wouldn't have been the same without it. To Matthew B. Doar: again, thanks for JDiff (http://javadiff.sourceforge.net), a great doclet for reporting API differences. The tool greatly helped me in finding the smaller changes in Java 6. For my Aunt Alicia and Uncle George O'Toole, thanks for watching after my dad.

Lastly, there's this crazy woman I've been with for close to 20 years now—my wife, Lisa. Thanks for everything. Our dog, Jaeger, too, whose picture you'll find in Chapter 4. Thanks Dad. Here's to another June with you in the hospital. Third time's a charm.

Introduction

So you like living on the bleeding edge and want to learn about Java 6, aka Mustang. Welcome. What you hold in your hands is a look at the newest features of the early access version of Mustang. Working through the early access releases from Sun, I've painfully struggled through the weekly drops and demonstrated the latest feature set to help you decide when or if it is time to move to Java 6. OK, maybe it wasn't that painful. In any case, many of these new features make the transition from Java 5 (or earlier) to Java 6 the obvious choice.

Who This Book Is For

This book is for you if you like diving headfirst into software that isn't ready yet, or at least wasn't when the book was written. While writing the material for the book, I assumed that you, the reader, are a competent Java 5 developer. Typically, developers of earlier versions of Java should do fine, though I don't go into too many details for features added with Java 5, like the enhanced for loop or generics. I just use them.

How This Book Is Structured

This book is broken into ten chapters and one appendix. After the overview in Chapter 1, the remaining chapters attack different packages and tools, exploring the new feature set of each in turn.

After Chapter 1, the next few chapters dive into the more standard libraries. Chapter 2 starts with the core libraries of java.lang and java.util. Here, you get a look at the new console I/O feature and the many changes to the collections framework, among other additions. Chapter 3 jumps into updates to the I/O, networking, and security features. From checking file system space to cookie management and beyond, you'll explore how this next set of libraries has changed with Java SE 6.0. Onward into Chapter 4, you'll learn about the latest AWT and Swing changes. Here, you'll jump into some of the more user-visible changes, like splash screen support and system tray access, table sorting and filtering, text component printing, and more.

With the next series of chapters, the APIs start becoming more familiar to the enterprise developer; though with Mustang, these are now standard with the Standard Edition.

Chapter 5 explores the JDBC 4.0 additions. You'll just love the latest in database driver loading that Mustang offers, among the many other additions for SQL-based database access. The latest additions related to XML come out in Chapter 6, with the Java Architecture for XML Binding (JAXB) 2.0 API, the XML Digital Signatures API, and the Streaming API for XML. Chapter 7 then moves into web services, but with a twist, since Mustang is the client side—so you aren't creating them, but using them.

Onward to the next semi-logical grouping, and you're into tools-related APIs. Reading Chapter 8, you get a look into the Java Compiler API, where you learn to compile source from source. From compiling to scripting, Chapter 9 talks about Rhino and the JavaScript support of the platform, where you learn all about the latest fashions in scripting engines. The final chapter, 10, takes you to the newest annotation processing support. From all the latest in new annotations to creating your own, you're apt to like or dislike annotations more after this one.

The single appendix talks about Mustang's early access home at `https://mustang.dev.java.net`, the licensing terms, and the participation model. It may be too late by the time this book hits the shelf, but early access participants have been able to submit fixes for bugs that have been annoying them since earlier releases of the Java platform. Sure, Sun fixed many bugs with the release, but it was bugs they felt were worthy, not necessarily those that were critical to *your* business.

By the time you're done, the Java Community Process (JCP) program web site (`www.jcp.org`) will be your friend. No, this book isn't just about the JSRs for all the new features—but if you need more depth on the underlying APIs, the JCP site is a good place to start, as it holds the full specifications for everything introduced into Mustang. Of course, if you don't care for all the details, you don't need them to use the APIs. That's what this book is for.

Prerequisites

This book was written to provide you, the reader, with early access knowledge of the Java 6 platform. While the beta release was released in February 2006, that release was based on a weekly drop from November 2005, with further testing. Much has changed with the Java 6 APIs since then. By the time the book went through the production process, most of the code was tested against the late May weekly snapshots from `https://mustang.dev.java.net`, drops 84 and 85. There is no need to go back to those specific drops—just pick up the latest weekly drop, as opposed to using the first beta release. If there is a second beta, that is also probably a good place to start, though it will be newer than what I tested with, and thus could have different APIs.

Sun makes available different versions of the Mustang platform. If you want to use Sun's VM, then your system should be one of the following:

- Microsoft Windows 2000, Server 2003, XP, or Vista

- Microsoft Windows AMD 64

- Solaris SPARC (8, 9, 10, or 11)

- Solaris x86 (8, 9, 10, or 11)

- Solaris AMD 64 (10 or 11)

- Linux (Red Hat 2.1, 3.0, or 4.0; SuSE 9, 9.1, 9.2, or 9.3; SuSE SLES8 or SLES 9; Turbo Linux 10 (Chinese/Japanese); or Sun Java Desktop System, Release 3)

- Linux AMD 64 (SuSE SLES8 or SLES 9; SuSE 9.3; or Red Hat Enterprise Linux 3.0 or 4.0)

For a full set of supported configurations, see http://java.sun.com/javase/6/webnotes/install/system-configurations.html.

Macintosh users will need to get Mustang from Apple. The Mac Java Community web site, at http://community.java.net/mac, serves as a good starting point. At least during the early access period in the spring, they were offering build 82 when Sun had 85 available, so they're a little behind, but the build was at least available for both PowerPC- and Intel-based Macs.

Downloading the Code

You can download this book's code from the Source Code area of the Apress web site (www.apress.com). Some code in this book is bound to not work by the time Java 6 goes into production release. I'll try my best to update the book's source code available from the web site for the formal releases from Sun, beta releases, and first customer ship (FCS).

Support

You can head to many places online to get technical support for Mustang and answers to general Java questions. Here's a list of some of the more useful places around:

- JavaRanch, at `www.javaranch.com`, offers forums for just about everything in the Big Moose Saloon.

- Java Technology Forums, at `http://forum.java.sun.com`, hosts Sun's online forums for Java development issues.

- developerWorks, at `www.ibm.com/developerworks/java`, is IBM's developer community for Java, which includes forums and tutorials.

- jGuru, at `www.jguru.com`, offers a series of FAQs and forums for finding answers.

- Java Programmer Certification (formerly Marcus Green's Java Certification Exam Discussion Forum), at `www.examulator.com/moodle/mod/forum/view.php?id=168`, offers support for those going the certification route.

While I'd love to be able to answer all reader questions, I get swamped with e-mail and real-life responsibilities. Please consider using the previously mentioned resources to get help. For those looking for me online, my web home remains `www.zukowski.net`.

CHAPTER 1

■■■

Java SE 6 at a Glance

What's in a name? Once again, the Sun team has changed the nomenclature for the standard Java platform. What used to be known as Java 2 Standard Edition (J2SE) 5.0 (or version 1.5 for the Java Development Kit [JDK]) has become Java SE 6 with the latest release. It seems some folks don't like "Java" being abbreviated, if I had to guess. Java SE 6 has a code name of Mustang, and came into being through the Java Community Process (JCP) as Java Specification Request (JSR) 270. Similar to how J2SE 5.0 came about as JSR 176, JSR 270 serves as an umbrella JSR, where other JSRs go through the JCP public review phase on their own, and become part of the "next" standard edition platform if they are ready in time.

The JSRs that are planned to be part of Mustang include the following:

- JSR 105: XML Digital Signature

- JSR 173: Streaming API for XML

- JSR 181: Web Services Metadata

- JSR 199: Java Compiler API

- JSR 202: Java Class File Specification Update

- JSR 221: JDBC 4.0

- JSR 222: JAXB 2.0

- JSR 223: Scripting for the Java Platform

- JSR 224: Java API for XML-Based Web Services (JAX-WS) 2.0

- JSR 250: Common Annotations

- JSR 269: Pluggable Annotation Processing API

With J2SE 5.0, the set of JSRs changed during the development and review process. One would expect the same with Mustang. Having said that, the blog of Mark Reinhold, who is the Mustang JSR specification lead, claims that won't be the case (see `http://weblogs.java.net/blog/mreinhold/archive/2005/07/mustang_compone.html`).

In addition to the announced set of JSRs, Mustang has a set of goals or themes for the release, as follows:

- Compatibility and stability

- Diagnosability, monitoring, and management

- Ease of development

- Enterprise desktop

- XML and web services

- Transparency

What does all this mean? As with J2SE 5.0, the next release of the standard Java platform will be bigger than ever, with more APIs to learn and with bigger and supposedly better libraries available.

Early Access

With Mustang, Sun has taken a different approach to development. While they still haven't gone the open source route, anyone who agreed to their licensing terms was permitted access to the early access software. Going through their `http://java.net` web site portal, developers (and companies) were allowed access to weekly drops of the software—incomplete features and all. APIs that worked one way one week were changed the next, as architectural issues were identified and addressed. In fact, developers could even submit fixes for their least favorite bugs with the additional source drop that required agreeing to a second set of licensing terms.

What does all this mean? There is apt to be at least one example, if not more, that will not work as coded by the time this book is printed and makes it to the bookstore shelves. For those features that have changed, the descriptions of the new feature sets will hopefully give you a reasonable head start toward productivity. For the examples that still work—great. You'll be able to take the example-driven code provided in this book and use it to be productive with Java SE 6 that much more quickly.

Everything in this book was created with various releases of the early access software to provide you with example after example of the new APIs. It is assumed that you have a reasonable level of knowledge of the Java programming language and earlier libraries, leaving the following pages to describe that which is being introduced into the next standard release of the Java Platform, Standard Edition.

Structure

After this first chapter, which provides an overview of what's new in Java SE 6, this book describes the new and updated libraries, as well as updates related to tools.

The initial chapters break up changes to the java.* and javax.* packages into logical groupings for explanation. Chapter 2 takes a look at the base language and utilities packages (java.lang.* and java.util.*). Chapter 3 is for input/output (I/O), networking, and security. Chapter 4 addresses graphical updates in the AWT and Swing work, still called the Java Foundation Classes (JFC). Chapter 5 explores JDBC 4.0 and JSR 221. Chapter 6 moves on to the revamped XML stack and the related JSRs 105, 173, and 222. Last for the libraries section, Chapter 7 is on client-side web services, with JSRs 181, 250, and 224.

The remaining chapters look at tools like javac and apt, and explore how they've grown up. Chapter 8 looks at the Java Compiler API provided with JSR 199. You'll look into new features like compiling from memory. Chapter 9 is about that other Java, called ECMAScript or JavaScript to us mere mortals. Here, JSR 223's feature set is explored, from scripting Java objects, to compilation, to Java byte codes of scripts. Finally, Chapter 10 takes us to JSR 269 with the Pluggable Annotation Processing API.

No, this book is not all about the JSRs, but they occasionally provide a logical structure for exploring the new feature sets. Some JSRs (such as JSR 268, offering the Java Smart Card I/O API, and JSR 260, offering javadoc tag updates) missed being included with Mustang for various reasons. JSR 203 (More New I/O APIs for the Java Platform), missed the Tiger release and won't be included in Mustang either.

What's New?

No single printed book can cover all the new features of Mustang. While I'll try to neatly break up the new features into the following nine chapters, not everything fits in so nicely. For starters, Table 1-1 identifies the new packages in Java SE 6.

Table 1-1. *New Mustang Packages*

Package	Description
java.text.spi	Service provider classes for java.text package
java.util.spi	Service provider classes for java.util package
javax.activation	Activation Framework
javax.annotation	Annotation processing support
javax.jws	Web services support classes
javax.jws.soap	SOAP support classes
javax.lang.model.*	For modeling a programming language and processing its elements and types
javax.script	Java Scripting Engine support framework
javax.tools	Provides access to tools, such as the compiler
javax.xml.bind.*	JAXB-related support
javax.xml.crypto.*	XML cryptography–related support
javax.xml.soap	For creating and building SOAP messages
javax.xml.stream.*	Streaming API for XML support
javax.xml.ws.*	JAX-WS support

This just goes to show that most of the changes are "hidden" in existing classes and packages, which, apart from the XML upgrade, keeps everyone on their toes. You'll learn about most of these packages in later chapters, along with those hidden extras.

JavaBeans Activation Framework

While most of these packages are described in later chapters, let's take our first look at Mustang with the java.activation package. This package is actually old, and is typically paired up with the JavaMail libraries for dealing with e-mail attachments. Now it is part of the standard API set and leads us to more than just e-mail.

What does the Activation Framework provide you? Basically, a command map of mime types to actions. For a given mime type, what are the actions you can do with it? The CommandMap class offers a getDefaultCommandMap() method to get the default command map. From this, you get the set of mime types with getMimeTypes(), and for each mime type, you get the associated commands with getAllCommands(). This is demonstrated in Listing 1-1.

Listing 1-1. *Getting the Command Map*

```java
import javax.activation.*;

public class Commands {
  public static void main(String args[]) {
    CommandMap map = CommandMap.getDefaultCommandMap();
    String types[] = map.getMimeTypes();
    for (String type: types) {
      System.out.println(type);
      CommandInfo infos[] = map.getAllCommands(type);
      for (CommandInfo info: infos) {
        System.out.println("\t" + info.getCommandName());
      }
    }
  }
}
```

Running this program displays the mime types and their commands in the default location.

```
image/jpeg
        view
text/*
        view
        edit
image/gif
        view
```

How does the system determine where to get the default command map? If you don't call `setDefaultCommandMap()` to change matters, the system creates an instance of `MailcapCommandMap`. When looking for the command associated with the mime type, the following are searched in this order:

1. Programmatically added entries to the `MailcapCommandMap` instance

2. The file `.mailcap` in the user's home directory

3. The file *<java.home>*`/lib/mailcap`

4. The file or resources named `META-INF/mailcap`

5. The file or resource named `META-INF/mailcap.default` (usually found only in the `activation.jar` file)

As soon as a "hit" is found for your mime type, searching stops.

■Note See the javadoc for the `MailcapCommandMap` class for information on the format of the `.mailcap` file.

Another thing you can do with the Activation Framework is map files to mime types. This is something your e-mail client typically does to see if it knows how to handle a particular attachment.

The program in Listing 1-2 displays the mime types that it thinks are associated with the files in a directory identified from the command line.

Listing 1-2. *Getting the File Type Map*

```
import javax.activation.*;
import java.io.*;

public class FileTypes {
  public static void main(String args[]) {
    FileTypeMap map = FileTypeMap.getDefaultFileTypeMap();
    String path;
    if (args.length == 0) {
      path = ".";
    } else {
      path = args[0];
    }
    File dir = new File(path);
    File files[] = dir.listFiles();
    for (File file: files) {
      System.out.println(file.getName() + ": " +
        map.getContentType(file));
    }
  }
}
```

The default implementation of the `FileTypeMap` class is its `MimetypesFileTypeMap` subclass. This does a mapping of file extensions to mime types. Theoretically, you could create your own subclass that examined the first few bytes of a file for its magic signature (for instance, 0xCAFEBABE for `.class` files). The output from running the program is dependent on the directory you run it against. With no command-line argument, the current directory is used as the source:

```
> java FileTypes /tmp
ack.jpg: image/jpeg
addr.html: text/html
alabama.gif: image/gif
alarm.wav: audio/x-wav
alex.txt: text/plain
alt.tif: image/tiff
```

With the JavaMail API, you would typically create a DataHandler for the part of the multipart message, associating the content with the mime type:

```
String text = ...;
DataHandler handler = new DataHandler(text, "text/plain");
BodyPart part = new MimeBodyPart();
part.setDataHandler(handler);
```

Under the covers, this would use the previously mentioned maps. If the system didn't know about the mapping of file extension to mime type, you would have to add it to the map, allowing the receiving side of the message to know the proper type that the sender identified the body part to be.

```
FileTypeMap map = FileTypeMap.getDefaultFileTypeMap();
map.addMimeTypes("mime/type ext EXT");
```

Desktop

This mapping of file extensions to mime types is all well and good, but it doesn't really support tasks you want to do with your typical desktop files, like printing PDFs or opening OpenOffice documents. That's where Mustang adds something new: the Desktop class, found in the java.awt package. The Desktop class has an enumeration of actions that may be supported for a file or URI: BROWSE, EDIT, MAIL, OPEN, and PRINT. Yes, I really did say that you can print a PDF file from your Java program. It works, provided you have Acrobat (or an appropriate reader) installed on your system.

The Desktop class does not manage the registry of mime types to applications. Instead, it relies on the platform-dependent registry mapping of mime type and action to application. This is different from what the Activation Framework utilizes.

You get access to the native desktop by calling the aptly named getDesktop() method of Desktop. On headless systems, a HeadlessException will be thrown. Where the operation isn't supported, an UnsupportedOperationException is thrown. To avoid the former exception, you can use the isHeadless() method to ask the GraphicsEnvironment if it is headless. To avoid the latter, you can use the isDesktopSupported() method to ask the Desktop class if it is supported before trying to acquire it.

Once you have the Desktop, you can see if it supports a particular action with the isSupported() method, as shown in the following code:

```
Desktop desktop = Desktop.getDesktop();
if (desktop.isSupported(Desktop.Action.OPEN)) {
  ...
}
```

This does *not* ask if you can open a specific mime type—it asks only if the *open* action is supported by the native desktop.

To demonstrate, the program in Listing 1-3 loops through all the files in the specified directory, defaulting to the current directory. For each file, it asks if you want to open the object. If you answer YES, in all caps, the native application will open the file.

Listing 1-3. *Opening Files with Native Applications*

```
import java.awt.*;
import java.io.*;

public class DesktopTest {
  public static void main(String args[]) {
    if (!Desktop.isDesktopSupported()) {
      System.err.println("Desktop not supported!");
      System.exit(-1);
    }
    Desktop desktop = Desktop.getDesktop();
    String path;
    if (args.length == 0) {
      path = ".";
    } else {
      path = args[0];
    }
    File dir = new File(path);
    File files[] = dir.listFiles();
    for (File file: files) {
      System.out.println("Open " + file.getName() + "? [YES/NO] :");
      if (desktop.isSupported(Desktop.Action.OPEN)) {
        String line = System.console().readLine();
        if ("YES".equals(line)) {
          System.out.println("Opening... " + file.getName());
          try {
```

```
            desktop.open(file);
          } catch (IOException ioe) {
            System.err.println("Unable to open: " + file.getName());
          }
        }
      }
    }
  }
}
```

■Note The `console()` method of the `System` class will be looked at further in Chapter 3, along with other I/O changes.

You can change the `open()` method call to either `edit()` or `print()` if the action is supported by your installed set of applications for the given mime type you are trying to process. Passing in a file with no associated application will cause an `IOException` to be thrown.

The `mail()` and `browse()` methods accept a `URI` instead of a `File` object as their parameter. The `mail()` method accepts `mailto:` URIs following the scheme described in RFC 2368 (`http://www.ietf.org/rfc/rfc2368.txt`). In other words, it accepts `to`, `cc`, `subject`, and `body` parameters. Passing no argument to the `mail()` method just launches the e-mail composer for the default mail client, without any fields prefilled in. Browser URIs arc your typical `http:`, `https:`, and so on. If you pass in one for an unsupported protocol, you'll get an `IOException`, and the browser will not open.

Service Provider Interfaces

One of the things you'll discover about the Mustang release is additional exposure of the guts of different feature sets. For instance, in Chapter 2, you'll see how the use of resource bundles has been more fully exposed. Want complete control of the resource cache, or the ability to read resource strings from a database or XML file? You can now do that with the new `ResourceBundle.Control` class. The default behavior is still there to access `ListResourceBundle` and `PropertyResourceBundle` types, but now you can add in your own types of bundles.

As another part of the better internationalization support, the `java.util` and `java.text` packages provide service provider interfaces (SPIs) for customizing the locale-specific resources in the system. That's what the new `java.util.spi` and `java.text.spi` packages are for. Working in a locale that your system doesn't know about? You can bundle in your own month names. Live in a country that just broke off from another that has its own new locale or different currency symbol? No need to wait for the standard platform to catch up. Want to localize the time zone names for the locale of your users? You can do that, too.

The LocaleServiceProvider class of the java.util.spi package is the basis of all this customization. The javadoc associated with the class describes the steps necessary to package up your own custom provider. Table 1-2 lists the providers you can create. They are broken up between the two packages, based upon where the associated class is located. For instance, TimeZoneNameProvider is in java.util.spi because TimeZone is in java.util. DateFormatSymbolsProvider is in java.text.spi because DateFormatSymbols is in java.text. Similar correlations exist for the other classes shown in Table 1-2.

Table 1-2. *Custom Locale Service Providers*

java.text.spi	java.util.spi
BreakIteratorProvider	CurrencyNameProvider
CollatorProvider	LocaleNameProvider
DateFormatProvider	TimeZoneNameProvider
DateFormatSymbolsProvider	
DecimalFormatSymbolsProvider	
NumberFormatProvider	

To demonstrate how to set up your own provider, Listing 1-4 includes a custom TimeZoneNameProvider implementation. All it does is print out the query ID before returning the ID itself. You would need to make up the necessary strings to return for the set of locales that you say you support. If a query is performed for a locale that your provider doesn't support, the default lookup mechanism will be used to locate the localized name.

Listing 1-4. *Custom Time Zone Name Provider*

```
package net.zukowski.revealed;

import java.util.*;
import java.util.spi.*;

public class MyTimeZoneNameProvider extends TimeZoneNameProvider {
  public String getDisplayName(String ID, boolean daylight,
      int style, Locale locale) {
    System.out.println("ID: " + ID);
    return ID;
  }
```

```
  public Locale[] getAvailableLocales() {
    return new Locale[] {Locale.US};
  }
}
```

All custom locale service providers must implement getAvailableLocales() to return the array of locales you wish to translate. The exact signature of the getDisplayName() method is dependent on what you are translating.

Defining the class is only half the fun. You must then jar it up and place it into the appropriate runtime extension directory.

To tell the system that you are providing a custom locale service provider, you need to configure a file for the type of provider you are offering. From the directory from which you will be running the jar command, create a subdirectory named META-INF, and under that, create a subdirectory with the name of services. In the services directory, create a file after the type of provider you subclassed. Here, that file name would be java.util. spi.TimeZoneNameProvider. It must be fully qualified. In that file, place the name of your provider class (again, fully qualified). Here, that line would be net.zukowski.revealed. MyTimeZoneNameProvider. Once the file is created, you can jar up the class and the configuration file.

```
> jar cvf Zones.jar META-INF/* net/*
```

Next, place the Zones.jar file in the lib/ext directory, underneath your Java runtime environment. (The runtime is one level down from your JDK installation directory.) You'll need to know where the runtime was installed. For Microsoft Windows users, this defaults to C:\Program Files\Java\jdk1.6.0\jre. On my system, the directory is C:\jdk1.6.0\jre, so the command I ran is as follows:

```
> copy Zones.jar c:\jdk1.6.0\jre\lib\ext
```

Next, you need to create a program that looks up a time zone, as shown in Listing 1-5.

Listing 1-5. *Looking Up Display Names for Time Zones*

```
import java.util.*;

public class Zones {
  public static void main(String args[]) {
    TimeZone tz = TimeZone.getTimeZone("America/Los_Angeles");
    System.out.println(tz.getDisplayName(Locale.US));
    System.out.println(tz.getDisplayName(Locale.UK));
  }
}
```

Compile and run the program. The first `println()` will look up the name for the US locale, while the second uses the UK locale. Only the first lookup should have any output with `ID:` at the beginning of the line:

```
> java Zones
ID: America/Los_Angeles
ID: America/Los_Angeles
ID: America/Los_Angeles
ID: America/Los_Angeles
America/Los_Angeles
Pacific Standard Time
```

With the four `ID:`s there, apparently it looks up the name four times before returning the string in the line without the leading `ID:`. It is unknown whether this is a bug in the early access software or proper behavior.

■**Caution** Errors in the configuration of the `LocaleServiceProvider` JAR will render your Java runtime inoperable. You will need to move the JAR file out of the extension directory before you can run another command, like `java` to run the example or `jar` to remake the JAR file.

Summary

Playground (1.2), Kestrel (1.3), Merlin (1.4), Tiger (5.0), Mustang (6), Dolphin (7); where do the names come from? With each release of the standard edition, the core libraries keep growing. At least the language level changes seem to have settled down for this release. I remember when the whole of Java source and javadocs used to fit on a 720-KB floppy disk. With this chapter, you see why you now require 50 MB just for the API docs and another 50 MB or so for the platform. Read on to the libraries and tools chapters to discover the latest features of the Java Standard Edition in Mustang.

In this next chapter, you'll learn about the changes to the language and utilities packages. You'll learn about what's new and different with `java.lang.*`, `java.util.*`, and all of their subpackages. You'll learn about everything from updates, to resource bundle handling, to the concurrency utilities; you'll also learn about lazy atomics and resizing arrays.

CHAPTER 2

■■■

Language and Utility Updates

Where does one begin? The key parts of the Java platform are the `java.lang` and `java.util` packages, so it seems logical that the exploration of Java 6 will start there. From a pure numbers perspective, `java.lang` and its subpackages grew by two classes (as shown in Table 2-1). `java.util.*`, on the other hand, grew a little bit more. Table 2-2 shows a difference of seven new interfaces, ten new classes, and one new `Error` class.

Table 2-1. *java.lang.* Package Sizes*

Package	Version	Interfaces	Classes	Enums	Throwable	Annotations	Total
lang	5.0	8	35	1	26+22	3	95
lang	6.0	8	35	1	26+22	3	95
lang.annotation	5.0	1	0	2	2+1	4	10
lang.annotation	6.0	1	0	2	2+1	4	10
lang.instrument	5.0	2	1	0	2+0	0	5
lang.instrument	6.0	2	1	0	2+0	0	5
lang.management	5.0	9	5	1	0+0	0	15
lang.management	6.0	9	7	1	0+0	0	17
lang.ref	5.0	0	5	0	0+0	0	0
lang.ref	6.0	0	5	0	0+0	0	0
lang.reflect	5.0	9	8	0	3+1	0	21
lang.reflect	6.0	9	8	0	3+1	0	21
Delta		0	2	0	0+0	0	2

Table 2-2. *java.util.* * Package Sizes*

Package	Version	Interfaces	Classes	Enums	Throwable	Total
util	5.0	16	49	1	20+0	86
util	6.0	19	54	1	20+1	95
util.concurrent	5.0	12	23	1	5+0	41
util.concurrent	6.0	16	26	1	5+0	48
...concurrent.atomic	5.0	0	12	0	0+0	12
...concurrent.atomic	6.0	0	12	0	0+0	12
...concurrent.locks	5.0	3	6	0	0+0	9
...concurrent.locks	6.0	3	8	0	0+0	11
util.jar	5.0	2	8	0	1+0	11
util.jar	6.0	2	8	0	1+0	11
util.logging	5.0	2	15	0	0+0	17
util.logging	6.0	2	15	0	0+0	17
util.prefs	5.0	3	4	0	2+0	9
util.prefs	6.0	3	4	0	2+0	9
util.regex	5.0	1	2	0	1+0	4
util.regex	6.0	1	2	0	1+0	4
util.spi	6.0	0	4	0	0+0	4
util.zip	5.0	1	16	0	2+0	17
util.zip	6.0	1	16	0	2+0	19
Delta		7	16	0	0+1	24

■**Note** In Tables 2-1 and 2-2, the Throwable column is for both exceptions and errors. For example, 2+0 means two Exception classes and zero Error classes.

Between the two packages, it doesn't seem like much was changed, but the changes were inside the classes. Mostly, whole classes or packages were not added; instead, existing classes were extended.

For `java.lang`, the changes include the addition of a `console()` method to the `System` class to access the system console for reading input, including passwords, and writing output. There's a new `isEmpty()` method in the `String` class, similar methods added to both `Math` and `StrictMath` for numeric manipulations, and new constants added to `Double` and `Float`. The `java.lang.management` changes are related to monitor locks, such as getting the map of all locked monitors and the IDs of deadlocked threads.

With `java.util`, the changes are a little more involved. The new `Deque` interface (pronounced *deck*) adds double-ended queue support. Sorted maps and sets add navigation methods for reporting nearest matches for search keys, thanks to the `NavigableMap` and `NavigableSet` interfaces, respectively. Resource bundles expose their underlying control mechanism with `ResourceBundle.Control`, so you can have resource bundles in formats other than `ListResourceBundle` and `PropertyResourceBundle`. You also have more control over the resource bundle cache.

On a smaller scale, there are some smaller-scale changes. The `Arrays` class has new methods for making copies; the `Collections` class has new support methods; `Scanner` gets a method to reset its delimiters, radix, and locale; and `Calendar` gets new methods to avoid using `DateFormat` for getting the display name of a single field.

One last aspect of `java.util` worth mentioning was first explored in Chapter 1. The `java.util.spi` and `java.text.spi` packages take advantage of a new service provider–lookup facility offered by the `Service` class. Without knowing it, you saw how to configure the service via the provider configuration file found under the `META-INF/services` directory.

In `java.util.concurrent`, you'll find concurrent implementations for `Deque` and `NavigableMap`. In addition, the `Future` interface has been extended with `Runnable` to give you a `RunnableFuture` or `RunnableScheduledFuture`. And in `java.util.concurrent.atomic`, all the atomic wrapper classes get `lazySet()` methods to lazily change the value of the instance. Even `LockSupport` of `java.util.concurrent.locks` adds some new methods, though it doesn't change much in terms of functionality.

For the record, nothing changed in the `java.math` package.

The java.lang Package

The `java.lang` package is still the basic package for the Java platform. You still don't have to explicitly import it, and—for those packages that actually changed with Java 6—it probably has the fewest of changes. You'll take a quick look at two of the changes to the package:

- Console input and output

- Empty string checking

System.console()

As first demonstrated in Chapter 1, the System class has a new console() method. It returns an instance of the new Console class of the java.io package. It provides support for reading from and writing to the system console. It works with Reader and Writer streams, so it works correctly with high-order byte characters (which System.out.println() calls would have chopped off). For instance, Listing 2-1 helps demonstrate the difference when trying to print a string to the console outside the ASCII character range.

Listing 2-1. *Printing High-Order Bit Strings*

```
public class Output {
  public static void main(String args[]) {
    String string = "Español";
    System.out.println(string);
    System.console().printf("%s%n", string);
  }
}
```

```
> java Output
Espa±ol
Español
```

Notice that B1 hex (±) is shown instead of F1 hex (ñ) when using the OutputStream way of writing to the console. The first chops off the high-order bit converting the underlying value, thus displaying ± instead of ñ.

Note The %n in the formatter string specifies the use of the platform-specific newline character in the output string. Had \n been specified instead, it would have been incorrect for the platforms that use \r (Mac) or \r\n (Windows). There are times when you want \n, but it is better to not explicitly use it unless you really want it. See Wikipedia, the online encyclopedia, for more information about newlines (http://en.wikipedia.org/wiki/Newline).

While output using Console and its printf() and format() methods is similar to what was available with Java 5, input is definitely different. Input is done by the line and supports having echo disabled. The readLine() method reads one line at a time with echo enabled, whereas readPassword() does the same with echo disabled. Listing 2-2 demonstrates the reading of strings and passwords. Notice how the input prompt can be done separately or provided with the readPassword() call.

Listing 2-2. *Reading Passwords*

```
import java.io.Console;

public class Input {
  public static void main(String args[]) {
    Console console = System.console();
    console.printf("Enter name: ");
    String name = console.readLine();
    char password[] = console.readPassword("Enter password: ");
    console.printf("Name:%s:\tPassword:%s:%n",
        name, new String(password));
  }
}
```

```
> java Input
Enter name: Hello
Enter password:
Name:Hello:      Password:World:
```

Empty Strings

The String class has a new isEmpty() method. It simplifies the check for a string length of 0. As such, the following code

```
if (myString.length() == 0) {
...
}
```

can now be written as the following:

```
if (myString.isEmpty()) {
...
}
```

As demonstrated by running the program in Listing 2-3, you still need to check whether the string is null before you can call isEmpty(); otherwise a NullPointerException is thrown.

Listing 2-3. *Checking for Empty Strings*

```
public class EmptyString {
  public static void main(String args[]) {
    String one = null;
    String two = "";
    String three = "non empty";
    try {
      System.out.println("Is null empty? : " + one.isEmpty());
    } catch (NullPointerException e) {
      System.out.println("null is null, not empty");
    }
    System.out.println("Is empty string empty? : " + two.isEmpty());
    System.out.println("Is non empty string empty? : " + three.isEmpty());
  }
}
```

Running the program in Listing 2-3 produces the following output:

```
> java EmptyString
null is null, not empty
Is empty string empty? : true
Is non empty string empty? : false
```

The java.util Package

The classes in the java.util package tend to be the most frequently used. They are utility classes, so that is expected. Java 6 extends their utilitarian nature by adding the Deque interface to the collections framework, throwing in search support with navigable collections, exposing the guts of resource bundles for those who like XML files, and even more with arrays, calendar fields, and lazy atomics. The following will be covered in the upcoming sections of this chapter:

- Calendar display names

- Deques

- Navigable maps and sets

- Resource bundle controls

- Array copies

- Lazy atomics

Calendar Display Names

The `Calendar` class is used to represent a point of time to the system. Through the `DateFormat` class, you can display the date or time in a locale-sensitive manner. As long as you display your dates and times with the help of `DateFormat`, users shouldn't be confused if they see 01/02/03, as they will know it means February 1, 2003, for most European countries, and January 2, 2003, for those in the United States. Less ambiguous is to display the textual names of the months, but it shouldn't be up to you to decide (or translate) and figure out the order in which to place fields. That's what `DateFormat` does for you. The runtime provider will then have to worry about acquiring the localization strings for the days of the week and months of the year, and the display order for the different dates and time formats (and numbers too, though those are irrelevant at the moment).

In the past, if you wanted to offer the list of weekday names for a user to choose from, there wasn't an easy way to do this. The `DateFormatSymbols` class is public and offers the necessary information, but the javadoc for the class says, "Typically you shouldn't use `DateFormatSymbols` directly." So, what are you to do? Instead of calling methods like `getWeekdays()` of the `DateFormatSymbols` class, you can now call `getDisplayNames()` for the `Calendar` class. Just pass in the field for which you want to get the names:

```
Map<String, Integer> names = aCalendar.getDisplayNames(
  Calendar.DAY_OF_WEEK, Calendar.LONG, Locale.getDefault());
```

The first argument to the method is the field whose names you want. The second is the style of the name desired: `LONG`, `SHORT`, or `ALL_STYLES`. The last argument is the locale whose names you want. Passing in `null` doesn't assume the current locale, so you have to get that for yourself. With styles, getting the long names would return names like `Wednesday` and `Saturday` for days of the week. Short names would instead be `Wed` and `Sat`. Obviously, fetching all styles would return the collection of both long and short names, removing any duplicates.

Table 2-3 lists the different fields that support display names.

Table 2-3. *Displayable Names of the Calendar Class*

Field
ERA
MONTH
DAY_OF_WEEK
AM_PM

What you get back is a Map, not an ordered List. Instead, the set of map entries returned has the key part be the name and the value part be the ordered position for that name. So, passing the returned map onto println() will display the following:

```
{Saturday=7, Monday=2, Wednesday=4, Sunday=1, Friday=6, Tuesday=3, Thursday=5}
```

Of course, you shouldn't use println() with localized names. For example, had the locale been Italian, you would have lost data, seeing

```
{sabato=7, domenica=1, gioved∞=5, venerd∞=6, luned∞=2, marted∞=3, mercoled∞=4}
```

instead of

```
{sabato=7, domenica=1, giovedì=5, venerdì=6, lunedì=2, martedì=3, mercoledì=4}
```

Notice the missing accented *i* (ì) from the first set of results.

In addition to getting all the strings for a particular field of the calendar, you can get the single string for the current setting with getDisplayName(int field, int style, Locale locale). Here, style can only be LONG or SHORT. Listing 2-4 demonstrates the use of the two methods.

Listing 2-4. *Displaying Calendar Names*

```
import java.util.*;

public class DisplayNames {
  public static void main(String args[]) {
    Calendar now = Calendar.getInstance();
    Locale locale = Locale.getDefault();
    // Locale locale = Locale.ITALIAN;
    Map<String, Integer> names = now.getDisplayNames(
      Calendar.DAY_OF_WEEK, Calendar.LONG, locale);
```

```
    // System.out.println(names);
    System.console().printf("%s%n", names.toString());
    String name = now.getDisplayName(Calendar.DAY_OF_WEEK,
      Calendar.LONG, locale);
    System.console().printf("Today is a %s.%n", name);
  }
}
```

```
> java DisplayNames
{Saturday=7, Monday=2, Wednesday=4, Sunday=1, Friday=6, Tuesday=3, Thursday=5}
Today is a Saturday.
```

Try out different calendar fields to see different results. If names are not available for the field asked, null would be returned from either method.

There is one additional noteworthy change in Mustang that is not related to calendar display names, but is nevertheless part of Calendar. When you get an instance of Calendar, if your locale is Japanese, with a language of "ja" and country and variant of "JP" (new Locale("ja", "JP", "JP")), you will get a JapaneseImperialCalendar class back, instead of a Gregorian one. The Japanese system supports era-based year numbering after the Meiji era, where an ERA of 1 is Meiji (since January 1, 1868), an ERA of 2 is Taisho (since July 30, 1912), an ERA of 3 is Showa (since December 26, 1926), and an ERA of 4 is Heisei (since January 8, 1989).

Listing 2-5 demonstrates the class. It creates the necessary calendar, shows that there are five named eras, displays the current year (17 for 2005), and displays the class name of the calendar implementation, where the results are shown after the source. You'll need a system configured for the Japanese runtime and fonts to see the Kanji characters.

Listing 2-5. *Using the New JapaneseImperialCalendar Class*

```
import java.io.*;
import java.util.*;

public class JapaneseCalendar {
  public static void main(String args[]) {
    Locale locale = new Locale("ja", "JP", "JP");
    Calendar now = Calendar.getInstance(locale);
    Console console = System.console();
    Map<String, Integer> names = now.getDisplayNames(
      Calendar.ERA, Calendar.LONG, locale);
    console.printf("%s%n", names);
```

```
        console.printf("It is year %tY of the current era%n", now);
        console.printf("The calendar class is: %s%n", now.getClass().getName());
    }
}
```

```
> java JapaneseCalendar
{??=1, ??=0, ??=3, ??=4, ??=2}
It is year 0017 of the current era
The calendar class is: java.util.JapaneseImperialCalendar
```

■Note The other custom `Calendar` implementation is a Buddhist calendar for Thai locales. This is not new with Mustang.

Deques

Deque is short for *double-ended queue* (again, pronounced like *deck*, not *de-queue*). While a queue supports adding from one end and removing from the other, double-ended queues support adding and removing from both, like a stack and queue combined. The `Deque` interface extends from the `Queue` interface introduced with Java 5, and is the latest addition to the Java Collections Framework. Implementations of the interface include `LinkedList`, `ArrayDeque`, and the concurrent `LinkedBlockingDeque`.

The `LinkedList` is the most typical usage of a deque. It grows without bounds and has quick add and remove operations at both ends. An `ArrayDeque` has no capacity restrictions either, and offers a wraparound index implementation for optimal performance. Neither implementation is threadsafe. If you need thread safety, that's where `LinkedBlockingDeque` comes in. The `LinkedBlockingDeque` class implements the `BlockingDeque` interface, which extends from `Deque`. The class can either be bounded or not. If no capacity is specified, its size limit is `Integer.MAX_VALUE`.

Adding elements to a deque is done with one of three methods: `void addFirst(E e)`, `void addLast(E e)`, and `boolean add(E e)`, where the last method is equivalent to `addLast()`. Lack of capacity causes an `IllegalStateException` to be thrown. There is also the concept of offering an element to be added with `boolean offer(E e)`, `boolean offerFirst(E e)`, and `boolean offerLast(E e)`. Unlike the case of adding elements with the add*XXX*() methods, if an item can't be added when offered, `false` is returned. The boolean returned from the `add()` method is always `true`, whereas the boolean returned from the `offer()` set of methods indicates the success or failure of the operation.

Removal of elements also has its pair of method sets: `remove()`, `removeFirst()`, and `removeLast()` for one set; and `poll()`, `pollFirst()`, and `pollLast()` for the other. The removeXXX() methods throw a NoSuchElementException when the deque is empty, whereas the pollXXX() methods return null when the deque is empty. You can even remove a specific object with boolean remove(Object o), boolean removeFirstOccurrence(Object o), and boolean removeLastOccurrence(Object o), though deques are meant for adding and removing from the ends only. Removing from the middle of a deque is apt to lead to performance degradation, though the operation will succeed.

Deque has six methods for examining elements: element(), getFirst(), and getLast(), with peek(), peekFirst(), and peekLast(). There is no get() method, as element() is the interface method inherited from Queue. The get methods are similar to removeXXX(), as a NoSuchElementException is thrown when the deque is empty. The peek methods, on the other hand, return null when empty. Of course, this means that if a deque allows the addition of null values, you won't be able to tell the difference between a null item at the end of the deque or nothing in the deque. But that is where the size() method comes in handy.

As a deque is doubly linked, you can traverse through the elements in either order, forward or backward. Use iterator() to go through from front to back, and descendingIterator() to go in the reverse order, from back to front. You cannot, however, access an element by position—at least not through the Deque interface. While LinkedList is an implementation of Deque, it supports indexed access through the List interface.

Here's what the whole interface looks like:

```
public interface Deque extends Queue {
    public boolean add(Object element);
    public void addFirst(Object element);
    public void addLast(Object element);
    public boolean contains(Object element);
    public Iterator descendingIterator();
    public Object element();
    public Object getFirst();
    public Object getLast();
    public Iterator iterator();
    public boolean offer(Object element);
    public boolean offerFirst(Object element);
    public boolean offerLast(Object element);
    public Object peek();
    public Object peekFirst();
    public Object peekLast();
    public Object poll();
    public Object pollFirst();
    public Object pollLast();
    public Object pop();
    public void push(Object element);
```

```
    public Object remove();
    public boolean remove(Object element);
    public Object removeFirst();
    public boolean removeFirstOccurrence(Object element)
    public Object removeLast();
    public boolean removeLastOccurrence(Object element);
    public int size();
}
```

Why use a deque? Deques are useful data structures for recursive problems, like searching through a maze or parsing source. As you move along a path, you save "good" spots, adding more data along the way while you think the path is good. If the path turns bad, you pop off the bad bits, returning to the last good spot. Here, you would be adding and removing from the same end, like a stack. Once you find your way through, you start back at the beginning to reveal the solution, which starts at the other end.

In lieu of creating a program that finds its way through a maze of twisty passages, all alike, Listing 2-6 demonstrates the use of Deque—or more specifically, LinkedBlockingDeque—with its capacity limits. It is certainly not the best use of a deque, but it demonstrates the API and what happens when you hit the capacity limit. If all you are doing is adding to one end and removing from the other, you should consider using a Queue implementation in the collections framework instead. The program here takes the 23 names for months (both short and long) and adds them to a six-element blocking deque, one at a time, to the head. In another thread, elements are removed from the head and tail of the deque, based on the number of elements currently in the collection.

Listing 2-6. *Using a Capacity-Limited LinkedBlockingDeque*

```
import java.io.*;
import java.util.*;
import java.util.concurrent.*;

public class Blocked {
  public static void main(String args[]) {
    Calendar now = Calendar.getInstance();
    Locale locale = Locale.getDefault();
    final Console console = System.console();
    final Map<String, Integer> names = now.getDisplayNames(
        Calendar.MONTH, Calendar.ALL_STYLES, locale);
    console.printf("Starting names: %s%n", names);
    final Deque<String> deque = new LinkedBlockingDeque<String>(6);
    try {
      // Fails as too many elements
```

```java
    // Still adds some
    deque.addAll(names.keySet());
  } catch (IllegalStateException e) {
    console.printf("Full: %s%n", e);
  }
  // Reset, remove those that fit
  deque.clear();
  // Add one at time to beginning of deque
  new Thread() {
    public void run() {
      Set<String> keys = names.keySet();
      Iterator<String> itor = keys.iterator();
      String element = null;
      while (itor.hasNext() || element != null) {
        if (element == null) {
          element = itor.next();
          console.printf("MapGot: %s%n",  element);
        }
        console.printf("Offering: %s%n", element);
        if (deque.offerFirst(element)) {
          console.printf("MapRemoving: %s%n", element);
          itor.remove();
          element = null;
        } else {
          try {
            Thread.sleep(250);
          } catch (InterruptedException ignored) {
          }
        }
      }
      // Done. Give time to process rest.
      try {
        Thread.sleep(3500);
      } catch (InterruptedException ignored) {
      }
      System.exit(0);
    }
  }.start();
  while (true) {
    if ((deque.size() % 2 == 1)) {
      // remove head
      console.printf("Remove head: %s%n", deque.pollFirst());
```

```
      } else {
        // remove tail
        console.printf("Remove tail: %s%n", deque.pollLast());
      }
      // Sleep between loops
      try {
        Thread.sleep(500);
      } catch (InterruptedException ignored) {
      }
    }
  }
}
```

As shown in Listing 2-7, running the program generates lots of output due to the printf() statements. Each time an element is fetched from the source map, removed from the source map, offered to the deque, or removed from the deque, an output line is generated. Notice how the act of offering happens multiple times while the deque is full.

Listing 2-7. *Output from a LinkedBlockingDeque Sample*

```
> java Blocked
Starting names: {Jun=5, March=2, December=11, April=3, November=10, September=8,
  October=9, Sep=8, Aug=7, Apr=3, May=4, June=5, Feb=1, Dec=11, Oct=9, Jan=0,
  Mar=2, Jul=6, August=7, January=0, February=1, July=6, Nov=10}
Full: java.lang.IllegalStateException: Deque full
MapGot: Jun
Offering: Jun
MapRemoving: Jun
MapGot: March
Offering: March
MapRemoving: March
MapGot: December
Offering: December
MapRemoving: December
MapGot: April
Offering: April
MapRemoving: April
MapGot: November
Offering: November
MapRemoving: November
MapGot: September
```

```
Offering: September
MapRemoving: September
MapGot: October
Offering: October
Remove tail: null
Offering: October
Remove tail: Jun
Offering: October
MapRemoving: October
MapGot: Sep
Offering: Sep
Offering: Sep
Remove tail: March
Offering: Sep
MapRemoving: Sep
MapGot: Aug
Offering: Aug
Offering: Aug
Remove tail: December
Offering: Aug
MapRemoving: Aug
MapGot: Apr
Offering: Apr
Offering: Apr
Remove tail: April
Offering: Apr
MapRemoving: Apr
MapGot: May
Offering: May
Offering: May
Remove tail: November
Offering: May
MapRemoving: May
MapGot: June
Offering: June
Offering: June
Remove tail: September
Offering: June
MapRemoving: June
MapGot: Feb
Offering: Feb
Offering: Feb
```

```
Remove tail: October
Offering: Feb
MapRemoving: Feb
MapGot: Dec
Offering: Dec
Offering: Dec
Remove tail: Sep
Offering: Dec
MapRemoving: Dec
MapGot: Oct
Offering: Oct
Offering: Oct
Remove tail: Aug
Offering: Oct
MapRemoving: Oct
MapGot: Jan
Offering: Jan
Offering: Jan
Remove tail: Apr
Offering: Jan
MapRemoving: Jan
MapGot: Mar
Offering: Mar
Offering: Mar
Remove tail: May
Offering: Mar
MapRemoving: Mar
MapGot: Jul
Offering: Jul
Offering: Jul
Remove tail: June
Offering: Jul
MapRemoving: Jul
MapGot: August
Offering: August
Offering: August
Remove tail: Feb
Offering: August
MapRemoving: August
```

```
MapGot: January
Offering: January
Offering: January
Remove tail: Dec
Offering: January
MapRemoving: January
MapGot: February
Offering: February
Offering: February
Remove tail: Oct
Offering: February
MapRemoving: February
MapGot: July
Offering: July
Offering: July
Remove tail: Jan
Offering: July
MapRemoving: July
MapGot: Nov
Offering: Nov
Offering: Nov
Remove tail: Mar
Offering: Nov
MapRemoving: Nov
Remove tail: Jul
Remove head: Nov
Remove tail: August
Remove head: July
Remove tail: January
Remove head: February
Remove tail: null
```

■Note There are 23 combined names for months between short and long because May counts for both the short and long name of the fifth month. Since getDisplayNames() returns a Map, May can't be the key for two entries, one short and one long.

Navigable Maps and Sets

Yet another new piece of the Java Collections Framework is the new NavigableMap and NavigableSet interfaces. They extend the SortedMap and SortedSet interfaces, respectively, to essentially add search options to the interfaces.

The NavigableMap Interface

For NavigableMap, there are essentially three sets of methods. One set of methods gets you submaps, another set works with the map entries, and the last set works with the map keys.

There are three methods in the first set. To start with, navigableHeadMap(toKey) returns a NavigableMap with all the keys up to, but not including, the toKey. Next, there is navigableTailMap(fromKey), which returns a NavigableMap with all the keys, starting with the fromKey, inclusive, to the end. Last, there is navigableSubMap(fromKey, toKey), which gives you a NavigableMap, starting with the fromKey, inclusive, to the toKey, exclusive. Always remember that the starting key is inclusive and the ending key is exclusive ([startKey, endKey)). Functionally, these methods are the same as the headMap(), tailMap(), and subMap() methods of SortedMap, but return a different type—NavigableMap— instead.

The second set of methods works with the keys of the map. With SortedMap, you have the methods firstKey() and lastKey() for getting the edge keys of the map. NavigableMap adds several other keys you can get, as follows:

- ceilingKey(key): Used for getting the first key of the map greater than or equal to the given key, or null if there is none

- floorKey(key): Used for getting the first key of the map less than or equal to the given key, or null if there is none

- higherKey(key): Used for getting the first key of the map strictly greater than the given key, or null if there is none

- lowerKey(key): Used for getting the first key of the map strictly less than the given key, or null if there is none

The third set of methods is probably the most useful. When working with a SortedMap or Map instance, in general, you would get the key and then look up its value. This last set of methods returns a Map.Entry instance instead of a key. Thus, you don't have to do the secondary lookup operation. So, there are six new methods for the new operations mentioned in the second set, as follows:

- `ceilingEntry(key)`: Used for getting the first entry of the map greater than or equal to the given key, or `null` if there is none

- `firstEntry()`: Used for getting the first entry of the map, or `null` if there is none

- `floorEntry(key)`: Used for getting the first entry of the map less than or equal to the given key, or `null` if there is none

- `higherEntry(key)`: Used for getting the first entry of the map strictly greater than the given key, or `null` if there is none

- `lastEntry()`: Used for getting the last entry of the map, or `null` if there is none

- `lowerEntry(key)`: Used for getting the first entry of the map strictly less than the given key, or `null` if there is none

There are two additional methods for fetching entries from the map and removing them in a single step. These provide an easy way to iterate through all the elements of a map without using an iterator. Depending upon the `Map` implementation, it is possible for the iterator to become stale if the underlying map changes while processing its elements. The two methods are as follows:

- `Map.Entry<K,V> pollFirstEntry()`: Gets the entry the with first key of the map and removes the entry from map, or returns `null` if the map is empty

- `Map.Entry<K,V> pollLastEntry()`: Gets the entry with the last key of the map and removes the entry from map, or returns `null` if the map is empty

Two other `NavigableMap` methods worth mentioning are `descendingKeySet()` and `descendingEntrySet()`. Where `keySet()` and `entrySet()` give you the set of keys in ascending order, the new `NavigableMap` methods work in reverse order.

There are two implementations of the `NavigableMap` interface in Java 6. The old `TreeMap` class has been retrofitted to extend from `NavigableMap` instead of `SortedMap`. In addition, a concurrent version of the interface is available with the `ConcurrentSkipListMap` class. For those unfamiliar with skip lists, they are a form of ordered linked lists that maintain parallel linked lists for speeding up search time. While the `TreeMap` structure is balanced and searches from roughly the middle of the list to find a key, the `ConcurrentSkipListMap` always starts at the beginning—but thanks to the secondary skip lists, it keeps its search time close to that of a binary search.

There is nothing fancy about using the `NavigableMap` interface. Listing 2-8 demonstrates its usage with a map of the days of the week. Output follows the source.

Listing 2-8. *Using the NavigableMap Interface*

```
import java.io.*;
import java.util.*;

public class Navigable {
  public static void main(String args[]) {
    Calendar now = Calendar.getInstance();
    Locale locale = Locale.getDefault();
    Console console = System.console();
    Map<String, Integer> names = now.getDisplayNames(
      Calendar.DAY_OF_WEEK, Calendar.LONG, locale);
    NavigableMap<String, Integer> nav = new TreeMap<String, Integer>(names);
    console.printf("Whole list:%n%s%n", nav);
    console.printf("First key: %s\tFirst entry: %s%n",
      nav.firstKey(), nav.firstEntry());
    console.printf("Last key: %s\tLast entry: %s%n",
      nav.lastKey(), nav.lastEntry());
    console.printf("Map before Sunday: %s%n",
      nav.navigableHeadMap("Sunday"));
    console.printf("Key floor before Sunday: %s%n",
      nav.floorKey("Sunday"));
    console.printf("Key lower before Sunday: %s%n",
      nav.lowerKey("Sunday"));
    console.printf("Key ceiling after Sunday: %s%n",
      nav.ceilingKey("Sunday"));
    console.printf("Key higher after Sunday: %s%n",
      nav.higherKey("Sunday"));
  }
}
```

```
> java Navigable
Whole list:
{Friday=6, Monday=2, Saturday=7, Sunday=1, Thursday=5, Tuesday=3, Wednesday=4}
First key: Friday       First entry: Friday=6
Last key: Wednesday     Last entry: Wednesday=4
Map before Sunday: {Friday=6, Monday=2, Saturday=7}
Key floor before Sunday: Sunday
Key lower before Sunday: Saturday
Key ceiling after Sunday: Sunday

Key higher after Sunday: Thursday
```

The NavigableSet Interface

NavigableSet works in a fashion similar to NavigableMap, but without key/value pairs. Two of the three sets of methods contained in NavigableMap are contained in NavigableSet as well. You can get a navigable subset with navigableHeadSet(toElement), navigableSubSet(fromElement, toElement), and navigableTailSet(E fromElement). Or you can get specific elements with ceiling(element), floor(element), higher(element), and lower(element). You can also get and remove elements with pollFirst() and pollLast(), and get a descendingIterator() in addition to the ascending iterator().

The implementation classes are a rejiggered TreeSet (which now implements NavigableSet instead of SortedSet) and a new ConcurrentSkipListSet. Under the covers, the ConcurrentSkipListSet uses a ConcurrentSkipListMap for all the work. The Set implementation just wraps the calls to a proxied Map, at least for now storing Boolean.TRUE for all the values.

Resource Bundle Controls

Resource bundles are the way to go when creating programs that need to deal with internationalization. Ignoring the fact that all programs should really be written that way from the start, Java developers have been stuck with .properties files with their a=b format (PropertyResourceBundle), or .java class files with their returning of a two-dimensional array from getContents() (ListResourceBundle) since the dawn of Java time back in 1995. Ten-plus years later, the world has moved to XML—but you couldn't have resource bundles in XML, until now, thanks to the new inner Control class of the ResourceBundle class. By creating your own ResourceBundle.Control subclass, you can customize many aspects of your resource bundle loading.

Minimally, to create your own control, you need to override two methods: getFormats() and newBundle(). With getFormats(), you need to return a List of String objects for the collection of formats you support. To support only XML, you could return a singleton List. If you want to combine XML with the set of preexisting formats, you would add XML to the List returned by the base Control class. There are class constants for the other possible lists: FORMAT_CLASS, FORMAT_PROPERTIES, and FORMAT_DEFAULT (for both). Listing 2-9 shows an implementation that supports only XML.

Assuming the arguments are valid and point to an XML format, the newBundle() implementation in the XMLResourceBundleControl class calls the toBundleName() and toResourceName() methods to build up the file name for the resource bundle based upon the base name, locale, and format. Assuming the resource file is found, the XML file of resources is read with the help of the loadFromXML() method of the Properties class in the created ResourceBundle subclass. The handleGetObject() method of the subclass does the actual lookup, while the getKeys() method returns an Enumeration of keys.

Listing 2-9. *Customizing Resource Bundle Loading*

```java
import java.io.*;
import java.net.*;
import java.util.*;

public class XMLResourceBundleControl extends ResourceBundle.Control {
  private static String XML = "xml";

  public List<String> getFormats(String baseName) {
    return Collections.singletonList(XML);
  }

  public ResourceBundle newBundle(String baseName, Locale locale,
      String format, ClassLoader loader, boolean reload) throws
        IllegalAccessException, InstantiationException, IOException {

    if ((baseName == null) || (locale == null) || (format == null) ||
        (loader == null)) {
      throw new NullPointerException();
    }
    ResourceBundle bundle = null;
    if (format.equals(XML)) {
      String bundleName = toBundleName(baseName, locale);
      String resourceName = toResourceName(bundleName, format);
      URL url = loader.getResource(resourceName);
      if (url != null) {
        URLConnection connection = url.openConnection();
        if (connection != null) {
          if (reload) {
            connection.setUseCaches(false);
          }
          InputStream stream = connection.getInputStream();
          if (stream != null) {
            BufferedInputStream bis = new BufferedInputStream(stream);
            bundle = new XMLResourceBundle(bis);
            bis.close();
          }
        }
      }
    }
    return bundle;
  }
```

```
  private static class XMLResourceBundle extends ResourceBundle {
    private Properties props;

    XMLResourceBundle(InputStream stream) throws IOException {
      props = new Properties();
      props.loadFromXML(stream);
    }

    protected Object handleGetObject(String key) {
      return props.getProperty(key);
    }

    public Enumeration<String> getKeys() {
      Set<String> handleKeys = props.stringPropertyNames();
      return Collections.enumeration(handleKeys);
    }
  }

  public static void main(String args[]) {
    ResourceBundle bundle =
      ResourceBundle.getBundle("Strings", new XMLResourceBundleControl());
    String string = bundle.getString("Key");
    System.out.println("Key: " + string);
  }
}
```

The `main()` routine of the class here demonstrates the use of the
`XMLResourceBundleControl`. You have to pass an instance of the class to the `getBundle()`
method of `ResourceBundle` to tell the system that the default way of loading resource
bundles ain't happening. Once you've gotten the bundle, its usage is the same as for a
`ListResourceBundle` or a `PropertyResourceBundle`. The XML file to demonstrate the
`XMLResourceBundleControl` is shown in Listing 2-10.

Listing 2-10. *The Strings.xml Resource Bundle*

```
<?xml version="1.0" encoding="UTF-8"?>
<!DOCTYPE properties SYSTEM "http://java.sun.com/dtd/properties.dtd">
<properties>
  <entry key="Key">Value</entry>
</properties>
```

Running the program then shows that the Key key produces a value of Value:

```
> java XMLResourceBundleControl
Key: Value
```

Not many people know this, but loaded resource bundles are cached by the system. Thus, the second time you fetch a bundle from the same class loader, the loading of the bundle is instantaneous, as it never left memory. If you wish to reset the cache and clear out loaded bundles, call the static clearCache() method of ResourceBundle. There is a second version of clearCache(), which accepts a ClassLoader for even further memory usage optimization.

Array Copies

The Arrays class is full of static methods for manipulating arrays. Prior to Java 6, you could convert an array to a List, sort it, do a binary search, check for equality, generate a hash code, and display its elements as a comma-delimited string. Mustang adds another operation you can perform: copy. Think of it as another approach to System.arraycopy(), which doesn't require you to explicitly allocate space for the new array before calling the method. You can copy part or all of the array from the beginning with one of the many versions of the copyOf() method, or from any part with copyOfRange(). Both methods allow you to make the size of the destination array larger or smaller than the original to grow or shrink the array.

Listing 2-11 demonstrates the use of copyOf() by making a copy of the command-line arguments and then changing the copy. Notice that the original array contents aren't affected when the copy is changed.

Listing 2-11. *Resizing Arrays*

```
import java.util.Arrays;

public class ArrayCopy {
  public static void main(String args[]) {
    System.console().printf("Before (original)\t%s%n", Arrays.toString(args));
    String copy[] = Arrays.copyOf(args, 4);
    System.console().printf("Before (copy)\t\t%s%n", Arrays.toString(copy));
    copy[0] = "egg";
    copy[1] = "caterpillar";
    copy[2] = "pupa";
    copy[3] = "butterfly";
```

```
    System.console().printf("After (original)\t%s%n", Arrays.toString(args));
    System.console().printf("After (copy)\t\t%s%n", Arrays.toString(copy));
  }
}
```

Running the program produces the following output:

```
> java ArrayCopy one two three
Before (original)      [one, two, three]
Before (copy)          [one, two, three, null]
After (original)       [one, two, three]
After (copy)           [egg, caterpillar, pupa, butterfly]
```

Lazy Atomics

Sun introduced the java.util.concurrent.atomic package to the masses with Java 5. It provides a series of classes that wrap access to primitives and objects for atomically getting, comparing, and setting their values. As the set operation may take longer than it would for a nonatomic variable, the atomic program may function a little more slowly. This can be expected, as you're restricting access to something (a variable in this case). There is now an unsafe way to set the value of an atomic variable through the lazySet() method of AtomicBoolean, AtomicInteger, AtomicIntegerArray, AtomicIntegerFieldUpdater, AtomicLong, AtomicLongArray, AtomicLongFieldUpdater, AtomicReference, AtomicReferenceArray, and AtomicReferenceFieldUpdater. If you don't mind the value not being set immediately—possibly even queuing up multiple updates if done quickly enough—use the new lazySet() method of these classes.

Summary

Learning the language and utility class changes are the first step toward learning about Mustang. In this chapter, you got your first glimpse into the new features of two key sets of libraries. From reading passwords from the console, to writing Unicode strings, you discovered the usefulness of the new Console class. With the utility packages, there are the additions to the collection framework with the new deque data structure and the navigable maps and sets support. You learned how to make custom resource bundle controls and how to display names for parts of the calendar. Last, you learned how to work with lazy atomic variables.

For the next chapter, there are the changes besides `Console` in the `java.io` package. You'll see what's new for `java.io` along with the latest additions to the `java.net` and `java.security` packages. From checking file system space to handling cookies and beyond, the latest Mustang feature sets are coming your way.

CHAPTER 3

■ ■ ■

I/O, Networking, and Security Updates

What's new with I/O, networking, and security? When talking about what's new with I/O, this shouldn't automatically take you to the new I/O package (java.nio), which isn't so "new" anymore. In addition to that package, you'll discover changes to the java.io, java.net, and java.security packages. Following the numerical approach shown in Chapter 2, Table 3-1 shows the growth of the java.io package, Table 3-2 shows the changes for java.net, and Table 3-3 shows the changes for java.security. There are changes in java.nio, but not with the addition of classes, interfaces, and so on—so no table there.

Table 3-1. *java.io.* Package Sizes*

Package	Version	Interfaces	Classes	Throwable	Total
io	5.0	12	50	16+0	78
io	6.0	12	51	16+1	80
Delta		0	1	0+1	2

Table 3-2. *java.net.* Package Sizes*

Package	Version	Interfaces	Classes	Enums	Throwable	Total
net	5.0	6	34	2	12+0	54
net	6.0	8	38	2	12+0	60
Delta		2	4	0	0+0	6

Table 3-3. *java.security.* Package Sizes*

Package	Version	Interfaces	Classes	Enums	Throwable	Total
security	5.0	12	50	1	16+0	79
security	6.0	13	52	1	16+0	82
security.acl	5.0	5	0	0	3+0	8
security.acl	6.0	5	0	0	3+0	8
security.cert	5.0	8	27	0	9+0	44
security.cert	6.0	8	27	0	9+0	44
security.interfaces	5.0	13	0	0	0+0	13
security.interfaces	6.0	13	0	0	0+0	13
security.spec	5.0	3	22	0	2+0	27
security.spec	6.0	3	22	0	2+0	27
Delta		1	2	0	0+0	3

With even fewer additions than in Chapter 2, these four packages add next to nothing to the core libraries. There are certainly adjustments to existing classes, too, but just not new classes and interfaces here. You can even throw in the java.rmi and javax.rmi packages, as there are even fewer changes with RMI (Remote Method Invocation) libraries.

The java.io Package

Outside of the Console class covered in Chapter 2, the only java.io package changes worth mentioning are changes to file system access and manipulation within the File class, and the deprecation of its toURL() method.

Personally, I've been playing in the J2ME space lately. One of the things you can do there is ask a file partition how much space is available. Prior to Mustang, this information was not available, short of forking off a subprocess to run a platform-specific command or adding in some native code. Now, in Java 6, you can find this out with getUsableSpace() and getTotalSpace(). Between the two, you can show how much space each file system has available and has in total. Listing 3-1 does this for each available file system partition.

Listing 3-1. *Checking Available File System Space*

```java
import java.io.*;

public class Space {
  public static void main(String args[]) {
    Console console = System.console();
    File roots[] = File.listRoots();
    for (File root: roots) {
      console.printf("%s has %,d of %,d free%n", root.getPath(),
          root.getUsableSpace(), root.getTotalSpace());
    }
  }
}
```

Obviously, the results depend upon your particular system. Here's what one particular run might look like:

```
> java Space
A:\ has 30,720 of 730,112 free
C:\ has 5,825,671,680 of 39,974,860,288 free
D:\ has 51,128,320 of 100,431,872 free
E:\ has 0 of 655,429,632 free
F:\ has 0 of 0 free
G:\ has 19,628,294,144 of 40,047,280,128 free
H:\ has 347,922,432 of 523,993,088 free
I:\ has 248,061,952 of 255,827,968 free
```

In addition to providing access to available file system space, Mustang adds support for manipulating the read/write/execute attributes of files. Before Java 6, there was canRead() and canWrite(). Now, in addition to canExecute(), there are also methods for setting the access bits with setReadable(), setWritable(), and setExecutable(). For each setter method, there are two versions. The first takes a boolean parameter and sets the state accordingly, assuming the permission check passes. The second version takes two boolean arguments. For those file systems that support separate permissions for owner and non-owner, you can restrict which set you are changing. If the underlying file system doesn't distinguish between the two, then the second argument is ignored, changing the access for all to the value of the first.

The last of the changes to the File class is the deprecation of the toURL() method. Someone finally realized that the toURL() method returns invalid URLs when a space is in the file system path. Now, the appropriate way to get a URL for a File is to get its URI with toURI(), and then convert the URI to a URL with the toURL() method. For example

```
URL url = aFile.toURL();
```

becomes

```
URL url = aFile.toURI().toURL();
```

Listing 3-2 demonstrates the difference.

Listing 3-2. *Getting a Proper URL from a File Object*

```
import java.io.*;
import java.net.*;

public class FileURL {
  public static void main(String args[]) throws MalformedURLException {
    Console console = System.console();
    File file = new File("The End");
    URL url1 = file.toURL();
    URL url2 = file.toURI().toURL();
    console.printf("Bad url  %s%n", url1);
    console.printf("Good url %s%n", url2);
  }
}
```

When you compile the program, you'll need to ignore the deprecation usage warning.

Now, notice the difference between the results when run on a file (or directory) with a space in its name.

```
> java FileURL
Bad url  file:/C:/revealed/code/ch03/The End
Good url file:/C:/revealed/code/ch03/The%20End
```

Note Another new feature that might be worth mentioning is the protected clearError() method of PrintStream and PrintWriter. Subclasses can call the method to reset the internal error state of the stream.

The java.nio Package

The `java.nio` package is extremely light on changes. The `Buffer` class has a handful of new methods for accessing the backing array. These are useful when integrating with native code to provide the native code direct access to the array. Beyond that, the package is relatively unchanged.

The java.net Package

C is for cookie; that's good enough for me. The `java.net` changes in Mustang are related to cookie handling. While Java 5 has a `CookieHandler` class, Java 6 adds `CookiePolicy` and `CookieStore` interfaces with `CookieManager` and `HttpCookie` classes.

When talking about cookies, we're talking about the HTTP variety, which store data on your system. The stored data enables the remote system to remember some information about you when you visit again. This allows the stateless HTTP protocol to support online shopping, or just to preserve login information so you don't have to log in with each visit, among many other good and bad possibilities.

The J2SE 5.0 `CookieHandler` formed the basis of managing cookies. That basis was an abstract class with no implementation, no storage mechanism, no storage policy, and nothing to store. That's where Java 6 comes in. The `CookieManager` class is the `CookieHandler` implementation. `CookieStore` is the storage mechanism. `CookiePolicy` offers a policy of accepting or rejecting cookies, and finally `HttpCookie` offers something to save.

Now that you know all the members of the family, let us explore why you might want to use them. Cookies are typically thought of when using a browser. Browsers make connections over the Web using HTTP, which stands for HyperText Transfer Protocol. When you type in something like `www.apress.com` into the address area of your web browser, the browser tells the web server what user agent it is using and what image formats it supports, and it of course asks for a page and reads the response. You can do the same with your own Java programs. Just open a socket connection to a host and talk HTTP. The issue comes about when you want to write your own browser. You have to personally create a way to verify whether a cookie is for the right site, save it in a cache you come up with, and be sure to properly set up the response with any cookies that were saved. Not an impossible task, and certainly easier with `CookieHandler`, but not a quickie job either if you want to get it right. To see how to use the new classes, let us first explore how to manage cookies with Java 5 without the new classes. Listing 3-3 is the main driver program.

Listing 3-3. *Using CookieHandler in Java 5*

```
import java.io.*;
import java.net.*;
import java.util.*;

public class Fetch5 {
  public static void main(String args[]) throws Exception {
    if (args.length == 0) {
      System.err.println("URL missing");
      System.exit(-1);
    }
    String urlString = args[0];
    CookieHandler.setDefault(new ListCookieHandler());
    URL url = new URL(urlString);
    URLConnection connection = url.openConnection();
    Object obj = connection.getContent();
    url = new URL(urlString);
    connection = url.openConnection();
    obj = connection.getContent();
  }
}
```

The key part of the Fetch5 program is highlighted. You call the setDefault() method of CookieHandler to install a handler. Unless there is long-term storage in the implementation, the first call to get the contents from a URL should have no locally stored cookies. The second call to get the contents will then have any cookies that were saved from the first run.

To create a CookieHandler, you have to implement its two abstract methods, get() and put():

- public Map<String,List<String>> get(URI uri, Map<String, List<String>> requestHeaders) throws IOException

- public void put(URI uri, Map<String, List<String>> responseHeaders) throws IOException

The get() method works on the request side. Are there any saved cookies to add to the request headers for the appropriate domain? The put() method is called when you get a response back from the server, letting you look at the response headers to see if there are any cookies. If any are present, you need to cache them off for the next get() call.

Implementing the put() method first tends to be more logical, as you don't yet know from where to get anything for the get() method.

To find the set of cookies, the put() method has a responseHeaders Map as a parameter. You need to find the set of map entries that are cookies, as follows:

```
List<String> setCookieList = responseHeaders.get("Set-Cookie");
```

■**Note** For simplicity here, we are only looking for Set-Cookie, not Set-Cookie2, in the response headers. RFC 2965 calls for the name change. The Java 6 classes are more complete, work with both, and conform with the RFC.

Once you have the list of cookies, you then have to loop through the list and save each cookie in a cache, represented by the variable cookieJar here. If a cookie already exists, you have to replace the existing one—you cannot have duplicates.

```
if (setCookieList != null) {
  for (String item : setCookieList) {
    Cookie cookie = new Cookie(uri, item);
    // Remove cookie if it already exists in cache
    // New one will replace it
    for (Cookie existingCookie : cookieJar) {
      ...
    }
    System.out.println("Adding to cache: " + cookie);
    cookieJar.add(cookie);
  }
}
```

First, the Cookie class here is something you need to create—there is no preexisting class in Java 5 for this. That's where HttpCookie comes into play with Java 6. Second, the cache is also something you have to come up with. In the example program here, it is just a List from the collections framework, but it could be an external MySQL database that preserves cookies between runs of the program. That is totally up to you in Java 5. With Java 6, the cache becomes the CookieStore.

There's a little more to the put() method, but you'll see the full version in the completed class. For now, let's see what there is to the get() method. The first part of get() is to find cookies from the cache that match the URI passed into the method. You need to create a comma-separated list of cached cookies.

```
// Retrieve all the cookies for matching URI
// Put in comma-separated list
StringBuilder cookies = new StringBuilder();
for (Cookie cookie : cookieJar) {
  // Remove cookies that have expired
  if (cookie.hasExpired()) {
    cookieJar.remove(cookie);
  } else if (cookie.matches(uri)) {
    if (cookies.length() > 0) {
      cookies.append(", ");
    }
    cookies.append(cookie.toString());
  }
}
```

After you have the comma-separated list, you have to make a Map to return. The Map must be read-only but has to start with the Map passed into get():

```
// Map to return
Map<String, List<String>> cookieMap =
  new HashMap<String, List<String>>(requestHeaders);

// Convert StringBuilder to List, store in map
if (cookies.length() > 0) {
  List<String> list = Collections.singletonList(cookies.toString());
  cookieMap.put("Cookie", list);
}
// Make read-only
return Collections.unmodifiableMap(cookieMap);
```

And that is really the whole of the class. Listing 3-4 is the CookieHandler implementation used for Java 5.

Listing 3-4. *Implementing a CookieHandler for Java 5*

```
import java.io.*;
import java.net.*;
import java.util.*;

public class ListCookieHandler extends CookieHandler {
```

```java
// "Long" term storage for cookies, not serialized so only
// for current JVM instance
private List<Cookie> cookieJar = new LinkedList<Cookie>();

public void put(URI uri, Map<String, List<String>> responseHeaders)
       throws IOException {

  System.out.println("Cache: " + cookieJar);
  List<String> setCookieList = responseHeaders.get("Set-Cookie");
  if (setCookieList != null) {
    for (String item : setCookieList) {
      Cookie cookie = new Cookie(uri, item);
      // Remove cookie if it already exists
      // New one will replace
      for (Cookie existingCookie : cookieJar) {
        if((cookie.getURI().equals(existingCookie.getURI())) &&
           (cookie.getName().equals(existingCookie.getName()))) {
          cookieJar.remove(existingCookie);
          break;
        }
      }
      System.out.println("Adding to cache: " + cookie);
      cookieJar.add(cookie);
    }
  }
}

public Map<String, List<String>> get(URI uri,
   Map<String, List<String>> requestHeaders) throws IOException {

  // Retrieve all the cookies for matching URI
  // Put in comma-separated list
  StringBuilder cookies = new StringBuilder();
  for (Cookie cookie : cookieJar) {
    // Remove cookies that have expired
    if (cookie.hasExpired()) {
      cookieJar.remove(cookie);
    } else if (cookie.matches(uri)) {
      if (cookies.length() > 0) {
        cookies.append(", ");
      }
```

```
        cookies.append(cookie.toString());
      }
    }

    // Map to return
    Map<String, List<String>> cookieMap =
      new HashMap<String, List<String>>(requestHeaders);

    // Convert StringBuilder to List, store in map
    if (cookies.length() > 0) {
      List<String> list =
        Collections.singletonList(cookies.toString());
      cookieMap.put("Cookie", list);
    }
    System.out.println("CookieMap: " + cookieMap);
    // Make read-only
    return Collections.unmodifiableMap(cookieMap);
  }
}
```

In Java 6, the ListCookieHandler turns into the CookieManager class. The cookieJar that is used as the cache becomes the CookieStore. One thing not in this implementation of CookieHandler is a policy for storing cookies. Do you want to accept no cookies, all cookies, or only cookies from the original server? That's where the CookiePolicy class comes into play. You will explore CookiePolicy more later.

The last part of the Java 5 situation is the Cookie class itself. The constructor parses out the fields from the header line. Listing 3-5 shows an implementation that will be replaced in Java 6 by HttpCookie. The Java 6 version will also be more complete.

Listing 3-5. *Implementing a Cookie Class to Save for Java 5*

```
import java.net.*;
import java.text.*;
import java.util.*;

public class Cookie {

  String name;
  String value;
  URI uri;
```

```java
String domain;
Date expires;
String path;

private static DateFormat expiresFormat1
    = new SimpleDateFormat("E, dd MMM yyyy k:m:s 'GMT'", Locale.US);

private static DateFormat expiresFormat2
    = new SimpleDateFormat("E, dd-MMM-yyyy k:m:s 'GMT'", Locale.US);

public Cookie(URI uri, String header) {
  String attributes[] = header.split(";");
  String nameValue = attributes[0].trim();
  this.uri = uri;
  this.name - nameValue.substring(0, nameValue.indexOf('='));
  this.value = nameValue.substring(nameValue.indexOf('=')+1);
  this.path = "/";
  this.domain = uri.getHost();

  for (int i=1; i < attributes.length; i++) {
    nameValue = attributes[i].trim();
    int equals = nameValue.indexOf('=');
    if (equals == -1) {
      continue;
    }
    String name = nameValue.substring(0, equals);
    String value = nameValue.substring(equals+1);
    if (name.equalsIgnoreCase("domain")) {
      String uriDomain = uri.getHost();
      if (uriDomain.equals(value)) {
        this.domain = value;
      } else {
        if (!value.startsWith(".")) {
          value = "." + value;
        }
        uriDomain = uriDomain.substring(uriDomain.indexOf('.'));
        if (!uriDomain.equals(value)) {
          throw new IllegalArgumentException("Trying to set foreign cookie");
        }
        this.domain = value;
      }
```

```java
      } else if (name.equalsIgnoreCase("path")) {
        this.path = value;
      } else if (name.equalsIgnoreCase("expires")) {
        try {
          this.expires = expiresFormat1.parse(value);
        } catch (ParseException e) {
          try {
            this.expires = expiresFormat2.parse(value);
          } catch (ParseException e2) {
            throw new IllegalArgumentException(
              "Bad date format in header: " + value);
          }
        }
      }
    }
  }

  public boolean hasExpired() {
    if (expires == null) {
      return false;
    }
    Date now = new Date();
    return now.after(expires);
  }

  public String getName() {
    return name;
  }

  public URI getURI() {
    return uri;
  }

  public boolean matches(URI uri) {

    if (hasExpired()) {
      return false;
    }
```

```
      String path = uri.getPath();
      if (path == null) {
        path = "/";
      }

      return path.startsWith(this.path);
  }

  public String toString() {
    StringBuilder result = new StringBuilder(name);
    result.append("=");
    result.append(value);
    return result.toString();
  }
}
```

At this point, you can actually run the Fetch5 program in Listing 3-3. To run the program, find a site that uses cookies and pass the URL string as the command-line argument.

```
> java Fetch5 http://java.sun.com
CookieMap: {Connection=[keep-alive], Host=[java.sun.com], User-Agent=[
  Java/1.6.0-rc], GET / HTTP/1.1=[null], Content-type=[
  application/x-www-form-urlencoded], Accept=[text/html, image/gif, image/jpeg,
  *; q=.2, */*; q=.2]}
Cache: []
Adding to cache: SUN_ID=141.154.45.36:196601132578618
CookieMap: {Connection=[keep-alive], Host=[java.sun.com], User-Agent=[
  Java/1.6.0-rc], GET / HITP/1.1=[null], Cookie=[
  SUN_ID=141.154.45.36:196601132578618], Content-type=[
  application/x-www-form-urlencoded], Accept=[text/html, image/gif,
  image/jpeg, *; q=.2, */*; q=.2]}
Cache: [SUN_ID=141.154.45.36:196601132578618]
```

The first line shows the adjusted map from the get() call. Since the cookie jar (cache) is empty when the initial get() is called, there are no cookie lines added. When the put() happens, a Set-Cookie header is found, so it is added to the cache. The next request to get() finds the cookie in the cache and adds the header to the adjusted map.

Now that you've seen the Java 5 way of caching cookies, let's change Listing 3-3 and the Fetch5 program to the Java 6 way. The following line

```
CookieHandler.setDefault(new ListCookieHandler());
```

changes to

```
CookieHandler.setDefault(new CookieManager());
```

Compile the program and you're done. No extra classes necessary. Listing 3-6 shows the modified version. As an additional step, the modified program shows the cookies cached to the store at the end of the run.

Listing 3-6. *Using CookieHandler in Java 6*

```java
import java.io.*;
import java.net.*;
import java.util.*;

public class Fetch {
  public static void main(String args[]) throws Exception {
    Console console = System.console();
    if (args.length == 0) {
      System.err.println("URL missing");
      System.exit(-1);
    }
    String urlString = args[0];
    CookieManager manager = new CookieManager();
    CookieHandler.setDefault(manager);
    URL url = new URL(urlString);
    URLConnection connection = url.openConnection();
    Object obj = connection.getContent();
    url = new URL(urlString);
    connection = url.openConnection();
    obj = connection.getContent();
    CookieStore cookieJar = manager.getCookieStore();
    List<HttpCookie> cookies = cookieJar.getCookies();
    for (HttpCookie cookie: cookies) {
      console.printf("Cookie: %s%n", cookie);
    }
  }
}
```

One difference between the Java 5 version created and the Java 6 implementation provided is that the CookieStore cache deals with the expiration of cookies. This shouldn't be the responsibility of the handler (CookieManager). All the handler needs to do is tell the cache to store something. The fact that other cookies have expired shouldn't matter to the handler.

Another difference is the CookiePolicy interface (not yet shown). You can define a custom policy for dealing with cookies or tell the CookieManager to use one of the predefined ones. The interface consists of a single method:

```
boolean shouldAccept(URI uri, HttpCookie cookie)
```

The interface also includes three predefined policies: ACCEPT_ALL, ACCEPT_NONE, and ACCEPT_ORIGINAL_SERVER. The last one will reject third-party cookies, accepting only those that come from the original server—the same server as the response.

To set the cookie policy for the CookieManager, call its setCookiePolicy() method the following:

```
CookieManager manager = new CookieManager();
manager.setCookiePolicy(CookiePolicy.ACCEPT_ORIGINAL_SERVER);
CookieHandler.setDefault(manager);
```

The CookieManager class also has a constructor that accepts a CookieStore and a CookiePolicy:

```
public CookieManager(CookieStore store, CookiePolicy cookiePolicy)
```

Use this constructor if you want to use a cache other than the in-memory CookieStore used as a default (such as for long-term cookie storage between runs). You cannot change the cache for the manager after creation, but you can change the default-installed handler at any time.

Besides the additional cookie support in standard Java, there is a new IDN class for converting internationalized domain names (IDNs) between an ASCII-compatible encoding (ACE) and Unicode representation. In addition, there is a new InterfaceAddress class and new methods added to NetworkInterface for providing information about the available network interfaces. Listing 3-7 demonstrates the new methods added. The method names make the purpose of the methods pretty obvious, so no explanation is necessary.

Listing 3-7. *Using NetworkInterface*

```
import java.io.*;
import java.net.*;
import java.util.*;
```

```java
public class NetworkInfo {
  public static void main(String args[]) throws SocketException {
    Console console = System.console();
    Enumeration<NetworkInterface> nets =
      NetworkInterface.getNetworkInterfaces();
    for (NetworkInterface netint : Collections.list(nets)) {
      console.printf("Display name: %s%n",
        netint.getDisplayName());
      console.printf("Name: %s%n", netint.getName());
      console.printf("Hardware address: %s%n",
        Arrays.toString(netint.getHardwareAddress()));
      console.printf("Parent: %s%n", netint.getParent());
      console.printf("MTU: %s%n", netint.getMTU());
      console.printf("Loopback? %s%n", netint.isLoopback());
      console.printf("PointToPoint? %s%n", netint.isPointToPoint());
      console.printf("Up? %s%n", netint.isUp());
      console.printf("Virtual? %s%n", netint.isVirtual());
      console.printf("Supports multicast? %s%n", netint.isVirtual());
      List<InterfaceAddress> addrs = netint.getInterfaceAddresses();
      for (InterfaceAddress addr : addrs) {
        console.printf("InterfaceAddress: %s --- %s%n",
          addr.getAddress(), addr.getBroadcast());
      }
      console.printf("%n");
    }
  }
}
```

Again, the results of running the program depend upon your system configuration. They're similar to what you might see with an `ipconfig` command. The physical address is shown as a series of signed bytes. More commonly, you would expect to see their hex values.

```
> java NetworkInfo
Display name: MS TCP Loopback interface
Name: lo
Hardware address: null
Parent: null
MTU: 1500
Loopback? true
PointToPoint? false
Up? true
```

```
Virtual? false
Supports multicast? false
InterfaceAddress: /127.0.0.1 --- /127.255.255.255

Display name: 3Com EtherLink PCI
Name: eth0
Hardware address: [0, 1, 2, 3, 4, 5]
Parent: null
MTU: 1500
Loopback? false
PointToPoint? false
Up? true
Virtual? false
Supports multicast? false
InterfaceAddress: /192.168.0.103 --- /192.168.0.255
```

The javax.net.ssl package should get a passing mention. There's a new SSLParameters class for encapsulating the SSL/TLS connection parameters. You can get or set these for an SSLSocket, SSLEngine, or SSLContext.

The java.security Package

As Table 3-3 previously showed, there aren't many added interfaces or classes in the security packages. The changes are related to some new methods added to the Policy class. The Policy class now has a new marker interface, Policy.Parameters, for specifying parameters when getting an instance. A second marker interface is Configuration. Parameters in the javax.security.auth.login package. These marker interfaces are implemented by the new URIParameter class, which wraps a URI for a Policy or Configuration provider. These are used internally by the PolicySpi and ConfigurationSpi classes, respectively, for what will become a familiar service provider lookup facility.

Summary

Keeping to the concept of building up from the basic libraries to those that are a tad more involved, in this chapter you looked at the I/O, networking, and security libraries. These packages stayed relatively unchanged. The File class finally has a free disk space API, and you can also manipulate the read, write, and execute bits. Cookie management is now available in a much simpler form with Java 6. You could certainly do things yourself with the API exposed in Java 5, but it is certainly easier the Mustang way. Last, you explored the new network interface to display newly available information.

The next chapter gets into some of the more visual new features of Mustang—those of the `java.awt` and `javax.swing` packages. You saw how to access the system desktop in Chapter 1. Chapter 4 teaches you about the new splash screen support, table sorting and filtering, and system tray access.

CHAPTER 4

■ ■ ■

AWT and Swing Updates

Have GUIs gotten better? Graphical user interfaces written with the Swing component set seem to be on the rise since JDK 1.4. I'm not sure what triggered the change, but it is no longer abnormal to see a full-fledged graphical program written from the ground up with the Java programming language. Just look at Sun's Swing Connection at www. theswingconnection.com to see the latest things people are doing with Java-based user interfaces. Of the packages covered in this book so far, the AWT and Swing packages have changed the most. Table 4-1 shows the java.awt updates, and Table 4-2 shows javax.swing's changes.

Table 4-1. *java.awt.* Package Sizes*

Package	Version	Interfaces	Classes	Enums	Throwable	Total
awt	5.0	16	90	0	4/1	111
awt	6.0	16	98	7	4/1	126
awt.color	5.0	0	5	0	2/0	7
awt.color	6.0	0	5	0	2/0	7
awt.datatransfer	5.0	5	5	0	2/0	12
awt.datatransfer	6.0	5	5	0	2/0	12
awt.dnd	5.0	5	17	0	1/0	23
awt.dnd	6.0	5	17	0	1/0	23
awt.event	5.0	18	25	0	0/0	43
awt.event	6.0	18	25	0	0/0	43
awt.font	5.0	2	16	0	0/0	18
awt.font	6.0	2	17	0	0/0	19
awt.geom	5.0	1	30	0	2/0	33
awt.geom	6.0	1	33	0	2/0	36

Continued

Table 4-1. *Continued*

Package	Version	Interfaces	Classes	Enums	Throwable	Total
awt.im	5.0	1	3	0	0/0	4
awt.im	6.0	1	3	0	0/0	4
awt.im.spi	5.0	3	0	0	0/0	3
awt.im.spi	6.0	3	0	0	0/0	3
awt.image	5.0	8	42	0	2/0	52
awt.image	6.0	8	42	0	2/0	52
awt.image.renderable	5.0	3	4	0	0/0	7
awt.image.renderable	6.0	3	4	0	0/0	7
awt.print	5.0	3	4	0	3/0	10
awt.print	6.0	3	4	0	3/0	10
Delta		0	12	7	0+0	19

Table 4-2. *javax.swing.* Package Sizes*

Package	Version	Interfaces	Classes	Enums	Throwable	Total
swing	5.0	24	119	1	1/0	145
swing	6.0	24	133	7	1/0	165
swing.border	5.0	1	9	0	0/0	10
swing.border	6.0	1	9	0	0/0	10
swing.colorchooser	5.0	1	3	0	0/0	4
swing.colorchooser	6.0	1	3	0	0/0	4
swing.event	5.0	23	23	0	0/0	46
swing.event	6.0	24	24	1	0/0	49
swing.filechooser	5.0	0	3	0	0/0	3
swing.filechooser	6.0	0	4	0	0/0	4
swing.plaf	5.0	1	47	0	0/0	48
swing.plaf	6.0	1	47	0	0/0	48
swing.plaf.basic	5.0	1	71	0	0/0	72
swing.plaf.basic	6.0	1	71	0	0/0	72
swing.plaf.metal	5.0	0	56	0	0/0	56
swing.plaf.metal	6.0	0	56	0	0/0	56

Package	Version	Interfaces	Classes	Enums	Throwable	Total
swing.plaf.multi	5.0	0	31	0	0/0	31
swing.plaf.multi	6.0	0	31	0	0/0	31
swing.plaf.synth	5.0	1	8	0	0/0	9
swing.plaf.synth	6.0	1	8	0	0/0	9
swing.table	5.0	4	7	0	0/0	11
swing.table	6.0	4	9	0	0/0	13
swing.text	5.0	21	79	0	2/0	102
swing.text	6.0	21	80	0	2/0	103
swing.text.html	5.0	0	30	1	0/0	31
swing.text.html	6.0	0	30	1	0/0	31
...text.html.parser	5.0	1	9	0	0/0	10
...text.html.parser	6.0	1	9	0	0/0	10
swing.text.rtf	5.0	0	1	0	0/0	1
swing.text.rtf	6.0	0	1	0	0/0	1
swing.tree	5.0	7	10	0	1/0	18
swing.tree	6.0	7	10	0	1/0	18
swing.undo	5.0	2	5	0	2/0	9
swing.undo	6.0	2	5	0	2/0	9
Delta		1	19	7	0+0	27

Just seeing the additions to the interface and class counts doesn't show the whole story for AWT and Swing. Besides just the additional interfaces and classes, many of the classes have internal changes, like additional methods. You'll find no new components added to either AWT or Swing, but plenty of changes to go around—all very visual.

The java.awt Package

You'll find the java.awt package growing to better integrate with the desktop environment. In addition to the Desktop class demonstrated in Chapter 1, you'll find other areas of the system environment exposed to the Java developer that were previously unavailable, as follows:

- Splash screen

- System tray

- Dialog modality

- GIF writer

- Text antialiasing

Splash Screens

For those who don't know what they are, splash screens are the graphics you see while a program is starting up. Most users like to see something happening quickly, and the graphic appeases the need for immediate feedback. Prior to Mustang, if you wanted any visual indication of your program loading, the Java runtime had to be fully started before you could create a screen to put in a temporary graphic while the rest of the program initialized. No more. In Mustang, you can now have the system display an initial graphic prior to the runtime becoming fully initialized.

The quick-and-dirty way of doing this is via the -splash command-line switch.

```
java -splash:MyImage.jpg HelloSplash
```

What happens here is the MyImage.png image will show immediately, centered in the screen. Once your application creates a top-level window, the image goes away. Supported image formats include GIF, JPEG, and PNG, including their animated, transparent, and translucent varieties.

It is that simple to do, though you typically don't want to force the user to specify a -splash command-line switch every time they start up your program. Instead, a better way to work with splash screens is to specify the splash screen in the manifest of a JAR file and jar up your application. To demonstrate, Listing 4-1 is a simple program that directly does absolutely nothing with splash screens.

Listing 4-1. *Creating a Simple GUI Window with a Label*

```java
import javax.swing.*;
import java.awt.*;

public class HelloSplash {
  public static void main(String args[]) {
    Runnable runner = new Runnable() {
      public void run() {
        try {
            Thread.sleep(3000);
        } catch (InterruptedException e) {
        }
```

```
        JFrame frame = new JFrame("Java 6 Revealed");
        frame.setDefaultCloseOperation(JFrame.EXIT_ON_CLOSE);
        JLabel label = new JLabel(
            " Java 6 Revealed", JLabel.CENTER);
        frame.add(label, BorderLayout.CENTER);
        frame.setSize(300, 95);
        frame.setVisible(true);
      }
    };
    EventQueue.invokeLater(runner);
  }
}
```

Compile and run the program with the earlier command-line switch to make sure everything works fine. Be sure you have an image available to use as the splash screen. When the program is run, your image will show first (as in Figure 4-1), and then the screen in Figure 4-2 will be shown.

Figure 4-1. *A splash screen of my dog, Jaeger*

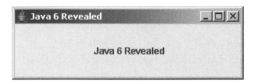

Figure 4-2. *A simple graphical screen*

To move this program into the world of JAR files, your manifest file needs to specify the main class to execute and the name of the image to display as the splash screen. The main class is specified using the Main-Class identifier, and the splash screen is specified with SplashScreen-Image. Create a file named manifest.mf, and place the contents of Listing 4-2 in it. Make corrections for the image name if you decide to name the image differently, possibly due to a different image file format.

Listing 4-2. *The Manifest File to Show the Splash Screen*

```
Manifest-Version: 1.0
Main-Class: HelloSplash
SplashScreen-Image: MyImage.jpg
```

Next, package up the manifest file, class files, and image.

```
jar -mcvf manifest.mf Splash.jar HelloSplash*.class MyImage.jpg
```

You can now run your program by passing the JAR file name to the `java -jar` command.

```
java -jar Splash.jar
```

Notice that you don't have to specify the `-splash` option here anymore to see the splash screen. This is the typical way that splash screens will be packed up for users.

For those interested in doing a little more with splash screens, you have access to the splash screen area in your program when the runtime starts up, but before you create your own window. For instance, if you want to change the image to indicate some level of progress, add a call to the `setImageURL()` method, as follows:

```
SplashScreen splash = SplashScreen.getSplashScreen();
URL url = ...;
splash.setImageURL(url);
```

The image specified by the URL should be the same size as the original, since the splash screen area doesn't grow based upon the new image provided. To find out its size, just ask with a call to `getSize()`, which returns a `Dimension` object. There are no borders around the splash screen image, so it should be the size of the original image specified as the splash screen.

If you want to show a progress bar over the splash screen, a little extra work is involved. You can think of the splash screen as a double-buffered image. You get its graphics context with the `createGraphics()` method, draw to it, and then tell the splash screen to update itself with its `update()` method. Until `update()` is called, the user doesn't see the intermediate drawing operations. So, for the "draw to it" part, you would draw a growing rectangle. The `Graphics` object returned from the `createGraphics()` method is a `Graphics2D` object, so more advanced graphics operations can be done. For simplicity's sake, Listing 4-3 only draws a growing white rectangle over the splash screen. Consider changing the color if white doesn't work with your image.

Listing 4-3. *Showing a Progress Bar Over the Splash Screen*

```java
import javax.swing.*;
import java.awt.*;

public class LoadingSplash {
  public static void main(String args[]) {
    Runnable runner = new Runnable() {
      public void run() {
        SplashScreen splash = SplashScreen.getSplashScreen();
        Graphics g = splash.createGraphics();
        if (splash != null) {
          // Draw growing rectangle / progress bar
          for (int i=0; i < 100; i++) {
            g.setColor(Color.WHITE);
            g.fillRect(50, 50, i, 25);
            if (splash.isVisible()) {
              splash.update();
            } else {
              break;
            }
            try {
              Thread.sleep(100);
            } catch (InterruptedException e) {
            }
          }
        }
        JFrame frame = new JFrame("Java 6 Revealed");
        frame.setDefaultCloseOperation(JFrame.EXIT_ON_CLOSE);
        JLabel label = new JLabel(
            " Java 6 Revealed", JLabel.CENTER);
        frame.add(label, BorderLayout.CENTER);
        frame.setSize(300, 95);
        frame.setVisible(true);
      }
    };
    EventQueue.invokeLater(runner);
  }
}
```

When Listing 4-3 is run, the user will see Figure 4-3, with the growing progress bar over the dog's face. Notice the isVisible() check in Listing 4-3. If the user happens to close the window, the program just breaks out of the for loop. If your program is still initializing when the user closes the window, there needs to be a check that happens before the program continues with its main operations. Be sure to pass the image name to be drawn over via the -splash option, as follows:

```
java -splash:MyImage.jpg LoadingSplash
```

Figure 4-3. *A splash screen with a progress bar*

■Note On a Microsoft Windows machine, pressing Alt+F4 will close the splash screen immediately. The key sequence only closes the splash screen; it doesn't terminate the application.

The final method of SplashScreen worth mentioning is the close() method. To close the screen and release its resources before an AWT (or Swing) window is shown, you can call this method. Calling isn't necessary, though, as the method will be called automatically when the top-level window becomes visible.

System Tray

Yet another new class in AWT that provides direct access to the user's desktop is the SystemTray class. In the notification area of your desktop (where you see little icons about what "system apps" are running, like your antivirus software, the coffee cup logo for the browser's Java runtime, and network connectivity indicators), more and more applications are vying for a little part of this space. (See Figure 4-4 for a view of this area in

Microsoft Windows.) Now, your Java programs can fight for their rights, too. As the system tray is shared by all applications running on a system, you shouldn't place every icon there; however, for those applications that require quick, immediate notifications and/or startup, this is a good place to put them, as you can have the icon flash or jump up and down to grab the user's attention. Your application can even offer the user the option of whether to add the icon to the tray.

Figure 4-4. *The Windows system tray area*

The SystemTray class uses the Singleton pattern to offer access to the single instance of the tray.

```
SystemTray tray = SystemTray.getSystemTray();
```

Of course, before you even get the tray, you must see if it is supported on the user's platform.

```
if (SystemTray.isSupported()) {
  SystemTray tray = SystemTray.getSystemTray();
} else {
  System.err.println("No system tray. Go home.");
}
```

While the tray is supported on Sun's runtimes for Microsoft Windows, Linux, and Solaris, it is possible that another platform might not support the tray immediately after the Java 6 release, but add support for such a feature later.

What can you do with SystemTray once you get its instance? Why, add TrayIcon objects to it, of course. A tray icon is an image with an associated tool tip and pop-up menu. Rest your mouse over the image and you'll see the tool tip. Click on the image with the appropriate mouse action and you'll see the pop-up menu. Of course, if you want to do much of anything, you have to add menu items and listeners, too.

Listing 4-4 shows a simple example of using a system tray and tray icon. The jpgIcon.jpg image comes from the demo area of the JDK. Feel free to use your own icon as the image. Any image format supported by the Java platform can be used, including user-created ones. It just has to be an Image object, with a capital I.

Listing 4-4. *Demonstrating a Simple System Tray*

```java
import javax.swing.*;
import java.awt.*;

public class SimpleTray {
  public static void main(String args[]) {
    Runnable runner = new Runnable() {
      public void run() {
        if (SystemTray.isSupported()) {
          SystemTray tray = SystemTray.getSystemTray();
          Image image = Toolkit.getDefaultToolkit().getImage("jpgIcon.jpg");
          PopupMenu popup = new PopupMenu();
          MenuItem item = new MenuItem("Hello, World");
          popup.add(item);
          TrayIcon trayIcon = new TrayIcon(image, "Tip Text", popup);
          try {
            tray.add(trayIcon);
          } catch (AWTException e) {
            System.err.println("Unable to add to system tray: " + e);
          }
        } else {
          System.err.println("No system tray available");
        }
      }
    };
    EventQueue.invokeLater(runner);
  }
}
```

Compiling and running the program will add another icon to the system tray. Rest your mouse over it to see the tool tip text, as shown in Figure 4-5. Right-click the tray icon to see the pop-up menu, as shown in Figure 4-6.

Figure 4-5. *Showing the icon and tool tip for a new system tray application*

Figure 4-6. *Showing the menu for a new system tray application*

It's simple so far, but there's much more you can do with the system tray and its icons. Yes, each of your applications can add multiple icons to the system tray. To make the SimpleTray application interesting, you should first have your application detect when the tray icon is added or removed from the system tray. The SystemTray class allows you to add a PropertyChangeListener to detect these operations. Its addPropertyChangeListener() method requires you to pass in the property name to watch for changes. In the case of SystemTray, that name is trayIcons.

```
tray.addPropertyChangeListener("trayIcons", propListener);
```

With the PropertyChangeListener, the old and new values you are told about make up the array of tray icons associated with the SystemTray. By checking the difference between the old and new values, you can see which specific TrayIcon was added, or just calculate the delta between the counts of the two if you only need to know whether the operation was an add() or a remove().

```
PropertyChangeListener propListener = new PropertyChangeListener() {
  public void propertyChange(PropertyChangeEvent evt) {
    TrayIcon oldTray[] = (TrayIcon[])evt.getOldValue();
    TrayIcon newTray[] = (TrayIcon[])evt.getNewValue();
    System.out.println(oldTray.length + " / " + newTray.length);
  }
};
```

Next, you need to detect when the user selects an item in the pop-up menu. Associate an ActionListener with the MenuItem operation for selection detection. This is no different than pre-JDK 6 code for pop-up menus. What is different is the action that you can perform. One operation specific to the TrayIcon is the displaying of specially formatted messages via calling the following displayMessage() method: public void displayMessage (String caption, String text, TrayIcon.MessageType messageType). Here, selecting the "Hello, World" menu item shows a caption of "Good-bye" and text message of "Cruel World."

```
MenuItem item = new MenuItem("Hello, World");
ActionListener menuActionListener = new ActionListener() {
  public void actionPerformed(ActionEvent e) {
    trayIcon.displayMessage("Good-bye", "Cruel World",
      TrayIcon.MessageType.WARNING);
  }
};
item.addActionListener(menuActionListener);
```

Figure 4-7 shows the warning message.

Figure 4-7. *Warning message shown on selection of system tray pop-up menu item*

The last argument to displayMessage() is an enumerated type of TrayIcon.MessageType elements—one of the following: ERROR, INFO, NONE, and WARNING.

Figures 4-8 through 4-10 show examples of ERROR, INFO, and NONE messages, respectively.

Figure 4-8. *An example of an ERROR message*

Figure 4-9. *An example of an INFO message*

Figure 4-10. *An example of a NONE message*

There's more to using SystemTray, though. In addition to associating a PropertyChangeListener with SystemTray, and associating an ActionListener with each MenuItem in PopupMenu, you can associate an ActionListener with TrayIcon itself. Then, when you "select" the tray icon (typically with a double-click operation), the ActionListener is notified. Here's a simple example that removes the tray icon from the system tray when the icon is selected:

```
ActionListener actionListener = new ActionListener() {
  public void actionPerformed(ActionEvent e) {
    tray.remove(trayIcon);
  }
};
trayIcon.addActionListener(actionListener);
```

■**Note** SystemTray also supports associating a MouseListener and MouseMotionListener with the component. There is default behavior assigned here, as in the case of showing the pop-up menu. You can add your own operation if you need to do something other than showing tool tip text or a pop-up menu.

Listing 4-5 combines all these operations into one example program.

Listing 4-5. *Demonstrating a System Tray That Responds to Selection*

```
import javax.swing.*;
import java.awt.*;
import java.awt.event.*;
import java.beans.*;

public class ActiveTray {
  public static void main(String args[]) {
    Runnable runner = new Runnable() {
      public void run() {
```

```
    if (SystemTray.isSupported()) {
      final SystemTray tray = SystemTray.getSystemTray();
      PropertyChangeListener propListener = new PropertyChangeListener() {
        public void propertyChange(PropertyChangeEvent evt) {
          TrayIcon oldTray[] = (TrayIcon[])evt.getOldValue();
          TrayIcon newTray[] = (TrayIcon[])evt.getNewValue();
          System.out.println(oldTray.length + " / " + newTray.length);
        }
      };
      tray.addPropertyChangeListener("trayIcons", propListener);
      Image image = Toolkit.getDefaultToolkit().getImage("jpgIcon.jpg");
      PopupMenu popup = new PopupMenu();
      MenuItem item = new MenuItem("Hello, World");
      final TrayIcon trayIcon = new TrayIcon(image, "Tip Text", popup);
      ActionListener menuActionListener = new ActionListener() {
        public void actionPerformed(ActionEvent e) {
          trayIcon.displayMessage("Good-bye", "Cruel World",
            TrayIcon.MessageType.WARNING);
        }
      };
      item.addActionListener(menuActionListener);
      popup.add(item);
      ActionListener actionListener = new ActionListener() {
        public void actionPerformed(ActionEvent e) {
          tray.remove(trayIcon);
        }
      };
      trayIcon.addActionListener(actionListener);
      try {
        tray.add(trayIcon);
      } catch (AWTException e) {
        System.err.println("Unable to add to system tray: " + e);
      }
    } else {
      System.err.println("No system tray available");
    }
  }
};
EventQueue.invokeLater(runner);
  }
}
```

One last tidbit worth mentioning is the getTrayIconSize() method of SystemTray. If you don't use a prefabricated image as the icon on the system tray, you can ask the system what size image to create. Then, just create a buffered image, draw on it, and pass it along to the TrayIcon constructor, as shown here:

```
Dimension dim = tray.getTrayIconSize();
BufferedImage bi = new BufferedImage(
    dim.width, dim.height, BufferedImage.TYPE_INT_RGB);
Graphics g = bi.getGraphics();
// then draw on image before associating with tray icon
TrayIcon trayIcon = new trayIcon(bi, text, popup);
```

Dialog Modality

Top-level pop-up windows in Java-speak are called dialog boxes. They aren't the main windows (frames) of an application; they're typically used to interact with a user—either to display a message or accept user input. Pre-Mustang, dialog boxes were by default modeless, with an option to be modal. When a dialog box was modal, other windows of the application were blocked from accepting input, unless the window had the dialog box as its owner. Once the user reacted to the dialog accordingly, by entering the input or just closing the dialog, input to other windows of the application became accessible again. That is basically the limitations of modality with predecessors to Mustang.

Along comes Java 6 and you have more options. No longer are you limited in scope to one level of modality (on or off). Now you have four distinct settings, defined by the new Dialog.ModalityType enumeration, whose types are shown in Table 4-3.

Table 4-3. *Dialog.ModalityType Enumeration*

Dialog.ModalityType
APPLICATION_MODAL
DOCUMENT_MODAL
MODELESS
TOOLKIT_MODAL

Before describing each of the modalities, it is important to talk about them in the context of their default settings and the set of Dialog and JDialog constructors, of which there are 14 and 16, respectively. The default modality is defined by the DEFAULT_MODALITY_TYPE constant of the Dialog class. Calling the setModal() method with a value of false is the obvious MODELESS setting, whereas calling it with a value of true sets the modality of that Dialog to DEFAULT_MODALITY_TYPE. DEFAULT_MODALITY_TYPE happens to equate to APPLICATION_MODAL. This keeps all historical code valid, although new code should use the new setModalityType() method instead. As far as the constructors go, if you don't explicitly specify a modality, the initial modality is DEFAULT_MODALITY_TYPE. If you specify a boolean modality, you get the same settings as calling setModal() with that boolean value. The last option is explicitly setting the modality, which has the obvious effect.

What do all the different types mean? The obvious one is MODELESS. That has the same effect as it did before Mustang. A modeless dialog box will not block input to any other window of the application. Another modal dialog box could block input to it, but a modeless one will have no effect on another. The APPLICATION_MODAL setting is the next to describe, as it equates directly to the modality behavior of pre-Mustang code. All windows of the application that does not have the modal dialog box in its owner hierarchy will be blocked from getting focus. This means that new windows that are created from the modal dialog can accept input, but new windows created from other preexisting windows cannot.

It's with the last two, DOCUMENT_MODAL and TOOLKIT_MODAL, that life gets interesting. DOCUMENT_MODAL allows you to have different sets of windows that are modal. For instance, you can have a modal application window that calls up a help window. Provided the help window has a different top-level window that is not part of the main application hierarchy, it can be modal and create other modal windows whose modality is separate from the main window and any modal dialogs the main window creates. This is a common need when utilizing the JavaHelp library, in which you always want to be able to interact with help, even when the current window is modal. However, it never worked right prior to support for DOCUMENT_MODAL, as they had different owner hierarchies. The last option is TOOLKIT_MODAL. Think of TOOLKIT_MODAL as APPLICATION_MODAL, but where the application is the browser. This typically allows one applet in a browser to be modal, blocking other applets from accepting input. This is because all the applets are loaded with the same system toolkit. Your applet must have AWTPermission.toolkitModality enabled for TOOLKIT_MODAL to work.

In addition to setting the modality type of a window, you can set the modal exclusion type via the setModalExclusionType() method of Window. This method accepts one of the three values from the Dialog.ModalExclusionType enumeration, shown in Table 4-4.

Table 4-4. *Dialog.ModalExclusionType Enumeration*

Dialog.ModalExclusionType
APPLICATION_EXCLUDE
NO_EXCLUDE
TOOLKIT_EXCLUDE

Basically, you can set the modality type for a dialog and the windows created with it as the owner. Then, you can specify that specific windows with the dialog owner can be excluded from that base modality setting. When the ModalExclusionType is set to the NO_EXCLUDE option for a window, you get the normal behavior, in which that window participates in the behavior based on the current modality type of the window. The other two options allow you to use a modality type, but say that specific windows can override the setting and always accept input focus. When the ModalExclusionType is APPLICATION_EXCLUDE, you don't have this window participate in the window modality at the application level. TOOLKIT_EXCLUDE, on the other hand, works with both application and toolkit modality. There is no way to have a window exclude behavior at the toolkit level, but not the application level.

Before using either the modality types or the exclusion option, you can ask the toolkit if either is supported. To discover whether a particular modality is supported, ask the boolean isModalityTypeSupported(Dialog.ModalityType modalityType) method. To discover if an exclusion type is supported, ask boolean isModalExclusionType➥ Supported(Dialog.ModalExclusionType modalExclusionType).

Now that you've read the long-winded version describing the Mustang modality features, the program in Listing 4-6 shows off dual frames using the DOCUMENT_MODAL setting. Each frame has a button that creates a document modal option pane, accepting input. The label of the selected button changes to the text entered when the option pane closes.

Listing 4-6. *Demonstrating Modality Types*

```
import javax.swing.*;
import java.awt.*;
import java.awt.event.*;

public class DualModal {
  public static void main(String args[]) {
    Runnable runner = new Runnable() {
      public void run() {
        JFrame frame1 = new JFrame("Left");
        JFrame frame2 = new JFrame("Right");
        frame1.setDefaultCloseOperation(JFrame.EXIT_ON_CLOSE);
        frame2.setDefaultCloseOperation(JFrame.EXIT_ON_CLOSE);
        JButton button1 = new JButton("Left");
        JButton button2 = new JButton("Right");
        frame1.add(button1, BorderLayout.CENTER);
        frame2.add(button2, BorderLayout.CENTER);
        ActionListener listener = new ActionListener() {
          public void actionPerformed(ActionEvent e) {
            JButton source = (JButton)e.getSource();
```

```
            String text = getNewText(source);
            if (!JOptionPane.UNINITIALIZED_VALUE.equals(text) &&
                  text.trim().length() > 0) {
              source.setText(text);
            }
          }
        };
        button1.addActionListener(listener);
        button2.addActionListener(listener);
        frame1.setBounds(100, 100, 200, 200);
        frame1.setVisible(true);
        frame2.setBounds(400, 100, 200, 200);
        frame2.setVisible(true);
      }
    };
    EventQueue.invokeLater(runner);
  }
  private static String getNewText(Component parent) {
    JOptionPane pane = new JOptionPane(
      "New label", JOptionPane.QUESTION_MESSAGE
      );
    pane.setWantsInput(true);
    JDialog dialog = pane.createDialog(parent, "Enter Text");
    // Uncomment line and comment out next to see application modal
    // dialog.setModalityType(Dialog.ModalityType.APPLICATION_MODAL);
    dialog.setModalityType(Dialog.ModalityType.DOCUMENT_MODAL);
    dialog.setVisible(true);
    return (String)pane.getInputValue();
  }
}
```

Notice how you can interact with the top-level dialog over each frame, but not the frame under either of them when the dialog is shown. Figure 4-11 shows the initial pair of frames. Figure 4-12 shows the two frames with their respective option panes showing. Changing the setModalityType() line to use APPLICATION_MODAL and rerunning the program won't allow you to interact with both option frames simultaneously. You need to finish using one before you can bring up the other.

Figure 4-11. *Initial frames without either input pop-up window*

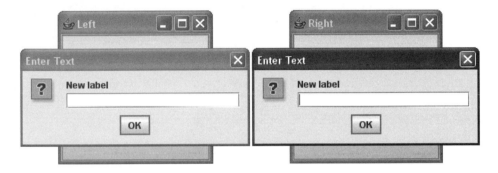

Figure 4-12. *Frames with both input pop-up windows showing*

■**Note** Changing the modality of a window that's already showing has no effect. You must hide the dialog box and make it visible again for the new modality setting to take effect.

One pre-Mustang feature is worth mentioning here: any AWT `Window` or subclass can request that it is always on top, via the `setAlwaysOnTop()` method of `Window`. This is not the same as modal and does not prevent other windows from getting input focus.

GIF Writer

Lempel-Ziv-Welch (LZW) is a lossless data compression algorithm implementation. Part of the GIF image format, it was originally patented by Sperry Corporation, and later taken over by Unisys. While displaying GIF formats has always been supported by the Java platform, the image I/O libraries only supported reading the format. Due to the aforementioned patent, support for writing GIF images was never part of the standard Java libraries. Now that the US patent and its counterparts around the globe have expired, support for writing GIF images is available, free of any legal threats or royalty requirements.

Listing 4-7 demonstrates the newly added capabilities.

Listing 4-7. *Writing GIF-Formatted Images*

```
import javax.imageio.*;
import java.io.*;
import java.awt.image.*;
import java.util.*;

public class ToGif {
  public static void main(String args[]) throws IOException {
    System.out.println("Supported Writer Formats:");
    System.out.println(Arrays.toString(ImageIO.getWriterFormatNames()));
    if (args.length == 0) {
      System.err.println("Missing input filename");
      System.exit(-1);
    }
    String name = args[0];
    File inputFile = new File(name);
    BufferedImage input = ImageIO.read(inputFile);
    File outputFile = new File(name+".gif");
    ImageIO.write(input, "GIF", outputFile);
  }
}
```

First, the program prints out a list of all available format names for writing images ([BMP, jpeg, bmp, wbmp, GIF, gif, png, JPG, PNG, jpg, WBMP, JPEG] for the Java 6 standard platform). Then, it checks for an image file name specified on the command line, reads it, and writes the converted image to GIF. The original file is not overwritten, even if it was originally a GIF image. Instead, .gif is simply appended to the entire original file name. For example, a file named HelloWorld.png would become HelloWorld.png.gif.

Text Antialiasing

I am not really into the specifics of describing antialiasing, so this description may not be the best from a technical standpoint; however, I nonetheless want to discuss this topic, since Java 6 adds some additional antialiasing support that benefits text.

Antialiasing is the smoothing-out of lines drawn into a graphics context (typically the screen, though also to a printer). As you know, the screen is just a bunch of square pixels. If you connect these pixels on a diagonal, the user will see what are known as "the jaggies," as shown in Figure 4-13. When enabled, antialiasing smoothes out these jagged edges by drawing a lighter shade of color around the pixel. As shown in Figure 4-14, your eyes don't perceive the jagged edges to be as bad with the added color around pixels. The difference is actually quite amazing when antialiasing is displayed at a proper pixel size, as opposed to the large size shown in Figures 4-13 and 4-14.

Figure 4-13. *The jaggies*

Figure 4-14. *Antialiased jaggies*

Now, step forward to Mustang, and you'll find LCD text antialiasing (where *LCD* means your LCD screen—more specifically, a flat-panel version to get optimal results). The prior form of antialiasing works great for grayscale printing. However, screens have their own display characteristics and can be even better optimized for improved display characteristics of text.

Instead of using gray scales to smooth out the edges, LCD text antialiasing involves splitting each pixel into its component types—namely three columns of light: red, green, and blue. It can then more gradually stagger the antialiasing columns to get a better result.

Figure 4-15 shows what Figure 4-14 would look like if each side pixel were split into its RGB components.

Figure 4-15. *Antialiased stripes*

The RGB values are taken with intensities of 75 percent for the outermost color (red on left, blue on right), 50 percent in the middle (green), and 25 percent on the inside (blue on left, red on right). Now, pixels aren't created through the specific drawing of the red, green, and blue colors. Instead, the value of each column is combined. This equates to a left color of 75-percent red, 50-percent green, and 25-percent blue (or roughly 191, 128, and 64; or an off-orange color). On the right side, you get 25-percent red, 50-percent green, and 75-percent blue, or a cyan-like color. Figure 4-16 shows this effect.

Figure 4-16. *LCD-antialiased jaggies*

When this LCD-antialiased line is scaled down to a normal size, your eyes somehow see this as blended to the right color mix, and don't even see any orange and light blue there.

To configure the system to perform this behavior, you must set the KEY_TEXT_ANTIALIASING rendering hint to one of the five available constants:

- VALUE_TEXT_ANTIALIAS_GASP

- VALUE_TEXT_ANTIALIAS_LCD_HRGB

- VALUE_TEXT_ANTIALIAS_LCD_HBGR

- VALUE_TEXT_ANTIALIAS_LCD_VRGB

- VALUE_TEXT_ANTIALIAS_LCD_VBGR

The first one, VALUE_TEXT_ANTIALIAS_GASP, equates to what you can think of as standard smoothing. This relies on a font designer–provided table to manipulate the font smoothing behavior. The last four describe subpixel configurations. For instance, Figure 4-15 shows the HRGB (horizontal red, green, blue) configuration. Which you choose depends upon your monitor's configuration. Also, if your monitor isn't an LCD display, don't expect the setting to have a good effect. You even have to match HRGB to an HRGB display, as something like VBGR in such a case will produce blurry text.

Miscellaneous Stuff

In addition to the bigger AWT changes just described, there are a handful of smaller changes worth mentioning. The Font class now has five new constants, one for each of the logical font families defined by the Java platform: SERIF, SANS_SERIF, MONOSPACED, DIALOG, and DIALOG_INPUT. No longer do you have to worry about typos in these names if you use the constants. The MouseEvent class now supports getting the absolute x and y coordinates of the event via its new methods getLocationOnScreen(), getXOnScreen(), and getYOnScreen(). The location is specified by a Point, while the x and y locations are specified by an int. Lastly, the AffineTransform class offers about a dozen new methods to support additional rotation options—many to better support quadrant rotations, like 90-, 180-, and 270-degree rotations.

The javax.swing Package

Mustang updates the javax.swing package to provide even better support for your graphic user interfaces. The changes include expanding the functionality of the existing components and bringing into the standard libraries a class that has been around in one form or another since the early days of the Java platform. The following list shows the new features of Swing to be highlighted:

- Table sorting and filtering

- The SwingWorker class

- JTabbedPane component tabs

- Text component printing

- Drag-and-drop support

Table Sorting and Filtering

With Java 6, Swing tables have grown up. The common functionality of sorting and filtering tables has finally been added to the standard functionality of a JTable. Through the help of a whole bunch of new classes and interfaces, your users get to click on a column to sort the elements in that column. In addition, you can offer them ways to easily filter the set of rows in a JTable to only the set that meets some criterion.

First off is the added sorting support. To sort a JTable, you need to associate a RowSorter class with the component. RowSorter is an abstract class that is responsible for mapping the original table model to the sorted version and back again. After an instance has been associated with the JTable, it is rarely interacted with directly.

DefaultRowSorter is a subclass of RowSorter that combines sorting and filtering support. You don't, however, typically use this class directly either. Instead, that's where TableRowSorter comes into play. It's a concrete implementation of the abstract DefaultRowSorter class. TableRowSorter is what you associated with the JTable to sort the shared model. The basic principle to enable sorting of a JTable is this simple:

```
TableModel model = ...;
JTable table = new JTable(model);
RowSorter sorter = new TableRowSorter(model);
table.setRowSorter(sorter);
```

Notice that the same model is passed into both constructors here: JTable and TableRowSorter. At this point, your table's rows can be sorted by a user clicking on a table column header, as shown in Figure 4-17 (before) and Figure 4-18 (after). The black arrow next to the Name header indicates that it is the sort key column. The arrow doesn't appear until a sort key column has been identified, which is why Figure 4-17 has none.

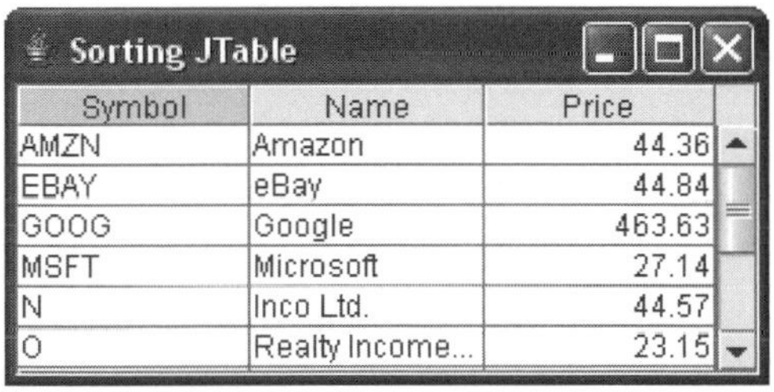

Figure 4-17. *Before sorting a JTable*

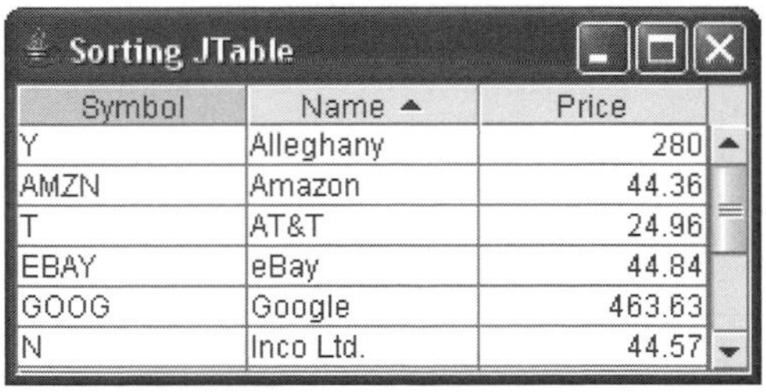

Figure 4-18. *After sorting a JTable*

Listing 4-8 demonstrates the sorting of a JTable. The table model offers a set of stock symbols, names, and prices, as shown in Figures 4-17 and 4-18.

Listing 4-8. *Sorting Table Elements*

```java
import javax.swing.*;
import javax.swing.table.*;
import java.awt.*;

public class SortedTable {
  public static void main(String args[]) {
    Runnable runner = new Runnable() {
     public void run() {
        JFrame frame = new JFrame("Sorting JTable");
        frame.setDefaultCloseOperation(JFrame.EXIT_ON_CLOSE);
        Object rows[][] = {
            {"AMZN", "Amazon", 44.36},
            {"EBAY", "eBay", 44.84},
            {"GOOG", "Google", 463.63},
            {"MSFT", "Microsoft", 27.14},
            {"N", "Inco Ltd.", 44.57},
            {"O", "Realty Income Corp.", 23.15},
            {"SUNW", "Sun Microsystems", 4.40},
            {"T",   "AT&T", 24.96},
            {"TIVO", "Tivo Inc", 5.45},
            {"X",   "US Steel", 49.54},
            {"Y", "Alleghany", 280.00}
          };
        String columns[] = {"Symbol", "Name", "Price"};
        TableModel model = new DefaultTableModel(rows, columns);
        JTable table = new JTable(model);
        RowSorter<TableModel> sorter =
          new TableRowSorter<TableModel>(model);
        table.setRowSorter(sorter);
        JScrollPane pane = new JScrollPane(table);
        frame.add(pane, BorderLayout.CENTER);
        frame.setSize(300, 150);
        frame.setVisible(true);
      }
    };
    EventQueue.invokeLater(runner);
  }
}
```

There is one key thing worth mentioning here. Clicking the last column will sort the table based on the last column value, as shown in Figure 4-19.

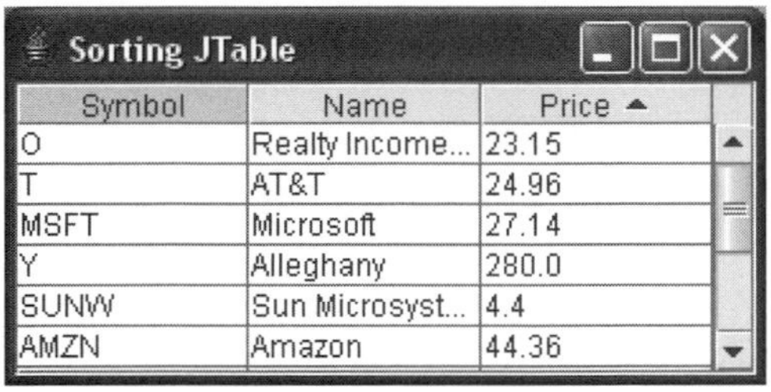

Figure 4-19. *An alphabetic sort of a numeric column*

Notice that the value 280.0 is between 27.14 and 4.4. By default, the elements of a DefaultTableModel are of type Object. In order to do numeric sorting, you have to change the data type of the column. This involves overriding the getColumnClass() method of DefaultTableModel:

```
TableModel model = new DefaultTableModel(rows, columns) {
  public Class getColumnClass(int column) {
    Class returnValue;
    if ((column >= 0) && (column < getColumnCount())) {
      returnValue = getValueAt(0, column).getClass();
    } else {
      returnValue = Object.class;
    }
    return returnValue;
  }
};
```

Here, the getColumnClass() method reports back that the data in the first row determines the class for all cells in that column. Thus, 280.0 would now be treated as type Number, not String, for sorting purposes. After the change, sorting the table in Figure 4-17 by the last column produces a more appropriate result, as shown in Figure 4-20.

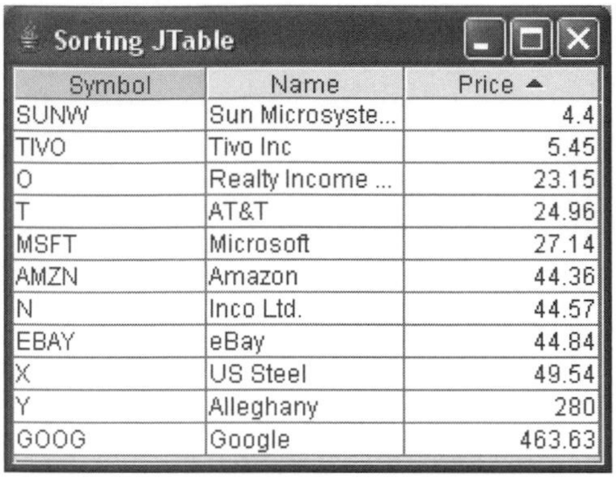

Symbol	Name	Price ▲
SUNW	Sun Microsyste...	4.4
TIVO	Tivo Inc	5.45
O	Realty Income ...	23.15
T	AT&T	24.96
MSFT	Microsoft	27.14
AMZN	Amazon	44.36
N	Inco Ltd.	44.57
EBAY	eBay	44.84
X	US Steel	49.54
Y	Alleghany	280
GOOG	Google	463.63

Figure 4-20. *A numeric sort of a numeric column*

Before moving on to filtering, it is important to mention the concept of selection. When sorting is enabled and the model has been reordered, selection of a row from the sorted model doesn't map back to the same row number in the source table model. That's where the `convertRowIndexToModel()` method comes into play. To demonstrate, the following code adds a `JButton` to the prior program that when selected displays the set of selected rows in the `JTable`:

```
JButton button = new JButton("Print Selected Rows");
ActionListener listener = new ActionListener() {
  public void actionPerformed(ActionEvent e) {
    for (int row: table.getSelectedRows()) {
      System.out.println("Selected row: " +
        table.convertRowIndexToModel(row));
    }
  }
};
button.addActionListener(listener);
frame.add(button, BorderLayout.SOUTH);
```

Without the call to `table.convertRowIndextoModel()`, printing the set of selected rows will print the set of selected rows for the current view of the model, whether sorted or otherwise. Once the conversion call is added, the selected row gets mapped back to the position in the original model. From here, you can print it, manipulate it, and so on. There is also another method, `convertRowIndexToView()`, which takes a row from the source table model and determines which row in the sorted model it maps to.

Tip To discover when a table-resorting operation happens, attach a `RowSorterListener` to `RowSorter` and implement the `sorterChanged()` method.

Filtering of table rows is done with the help of the abstract `RowFilter` class. You typically don't create your own subclasses of this, but instead use one of its six static methods to get a sufficient filter:

- `andFilter(Iterable<? extends RowFilter<? super M,? super I>> filters)`

- `dateFilter(RowFilter.ComparisonType type, Date date, int... indices)`

- `notFilter(RowFilter<M,I> filter)`

- `numberFilter(RowFilter.ComparisonType type, Number number, int... indices)`

- `orFilter(Iterable<? extends RowFilter<? super M,? super I>> filters)`

- `regexFilter(String regex, int... indices)`

The `andFilter()`, `orFilter()`, and `notFilter()` methods are themselves only for combining with other `RowFilter` instances. Want to check for a date greater than December 25, 2000, and a number less than 25? You'll need to combine the date filter and number filter with the help of the `andFilter()` method. It's that simple.

`RowFilter.ComparisonType` allows you to check for equality, inequality, before, and after type comparisons. The date or number provided fills in the other side of the equation. What the last `indices` argument buys you is the ability to limit the search to only the set of columns specified. Specifying no indices means everything will be searched.

Probably the most interesting of all the filters is the regular expression filter, or regex filter for short. This allows you to limit the visible view of the table model to those that match the specified regular expression (for instance, only those rows with a *T* in them). Figure 4-21 shows what happens after a table is filtered. The source listing follows in Listing 4-9.

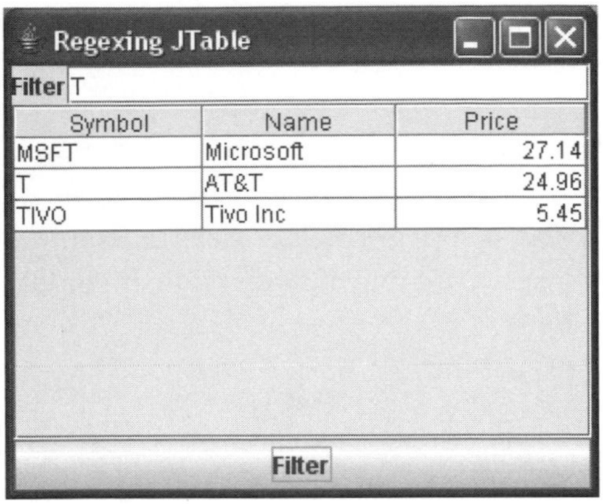

Figure 4-21. *Filtered table entries*

Listing 4-9. *Filtering Table Elements*

```java
import javax.swing.*;
import javax.swing.table.*;
import java.awt.*;
import java.awt.event.*;

public class RegexTable {
  public static void main(String args[]) {
    Runnable runner = new Runnable() {
     public void run() {
        JFrame frame = new JFrame("Regexing JTable");
        frame.setDefaultCloseOperation(JFrame.EXIT_ON_CLOSE);
        Object rows[][] = {
            {"AMZN", "Amazon", 44.36},
            {"EBAY", "eBay", 44.84},
            {"GOOG", "Google", 463.63},
            {"MSFT", "Microsoft", 27.14},
            {"N", "Inco Ltd.", 44.57},
            {"O", "Realty Income Corp.", 23.15},
            {"SUNW", "Sun Microsystems", 4.40},
            {"T",   "AT&T", 24.96},
            {"TIVO", "Tivo Inc", 5.45},
            {"X",   "US Steel", 49.54},
            {"Y", "Alleghany", 280.00}
          };
        String columns[] = {"Symbol", "Name", "Price"};
        TableModel model = new DefaultTableModel(rows, columns) {
```

```java
      public Class getColumnClass(int column) {
        Class returnValue;
        if ((column >= 0) && (column < getColumnCount())) {
          returnValue = getValueAt(0, column).getClass();
        } else {
          returnValue = Object.class;
        }
        return returnValue;
      }
    };

    final JTable table = new JTable(model);
    final TableRowSorter<TableModel> sorter =
      new TableRowSorter<TableModel>(model);
    table.setRowSorter(sorter);
    JScrollPane pane = new JScrollPane(table);
    frame.add(pane, BorderLayout.CENTER);

    JPanel panel = new JPanel(new BorderLayout());
    JLabel label = new JLabel("Filter");
    panel.add(label, BorderLayout.WEST);
    final JTextField filterText = new JTextField("T");
    panel.add(filterText, BorderLayout.CENTER);
    frame.add(panel, BorderLayout.NORTH);
    JButton button = new JButton("Filter");
    button.addActionListener(new ActionListener() {
      public void actionPerformed(ActionEvent e) {
        String text = filterText.getText();
        if (text.length() == 0) {
          sorter.setRowFilter(null);
        } else {
          sorter.setRowFilter(RowFilter.regexFilter(text));
        }
      }
    });
    frame.add(button, BorderLayout.SOUTH);
    frame.setSize(300, 250);
    frame.setVisible(true);
  }
};
EventQueue.invokeLater(runner);
}
}
```

Clicking a filtered table's column header still allows you to sort the rows, as demonstrated in Figure 4-22.

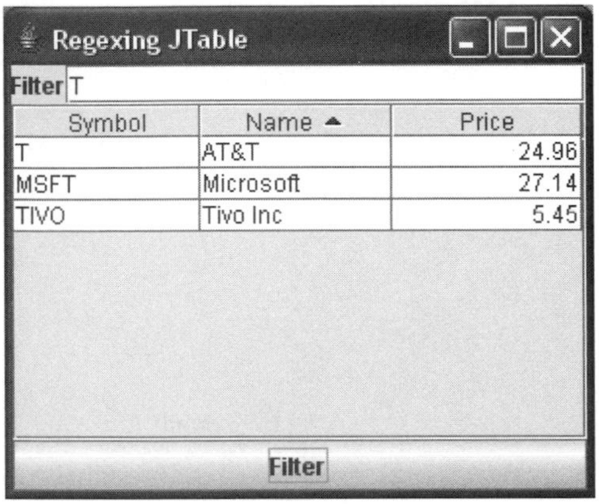

Figure 4-22. *A sorted and filtered JTable*

The SwingWorker Class

What's old is new again with SwingWorker. If the name sounds familiar, that's because the original version of this class first came about in the late 1990s. If you're familiar with the class, great—you should be able to get up to speed with it quickly. One major difference is that the class now implements Runnable, among other interfaces. There are more changes than that, though. What the SwingWorker class allows you to do is some background operation off the event dispatch thread, and then automatic completion on the event dispatch thread to update any screen state. Think of an operation like reading a file. This should not be done on the event thread because it takes some time, and you don't want to block the event thread while reading the file. Once you're done reading the file, you need to update the screen with some piece of data, like the number of characters in the file or the file contents. Why the separation? Basically, because you do this combined set of tasks frequently. (And if you don't, you should.) Remember that Swing components are not threadsafe, and should only be accessed from the event dispatch thread.

Without using the SwingWorker class, the normal mode of operation is to kick off a new thread that performs a lengthy task, and then when done, notify the event thread to update the screen of your changes. Sometimes you forget about the first piece of this, causing the event thread to block during the lengthy task. If you use SwingWorker, though, you can save yourself some trouble.

There are multiple ways to use the SwingWorker class. The basic operation, which follows the pattern previously mentioned, is the method pair doInBackground() and done(). You subclass SwingWorker, override the doInBackground() method with some lengthy operation, and override the done() method to do the last little bit of work, updating the Swing component from the event thread.

```
final JLabel label = new JLabel("Welcome");
SwingWorker worker = new SwingWorker() {
  public String doInBackground() {
    return "Lengthy task output";
  }
  public void done() {
    label.setText(get());
  }
}.execute();
```

The get() call here indirectly returns the value returned by doInBackground(). Until you call the execute() method, nothing is done yet as far as the thread actually running.

Tip The SwingWorker class has an enumeration for its StateValue. This can be one of DONE, PENDING, or STARTED. To get the current value, call the getState() method of SwingWorker.

The second way to use SwingWorker is with the publish() and process() pair of methods. These are appropriate when you need to pass off intermediate results while additional work is waiting to be processed. For instance, in the doInBackground() method, you might periodically call publish() to notify any waiting processes of something to process. The process() method then gets called here, which offers a way to perform intermediate steps on the event dispatch thread. Think of updating a JProgressBar here. Every once in a while, you need to push the progress bar along until completion, as shown in the following snippet of code:

```
public String doInBackground() {
  while (!done) {
    nextString = getNextString();
    publish(nextString);
    count++
    if (count >= 100) {
        done == true;
    }
    setProgress(100 * count / total)
  }
}
```

Along with calling the publish() method periodically, the doInBackground() method immediately notifies any property change listeners. Whether you need them or not is up to you. And the previously mentioned progress() method is still available for usage.

JTabbedPane Component Tabs

The JTabbedPane component offers a convenient way to show lots of stuff in a small amount of space. It does this by breaking the information into separate tabs. Select one tab to see a particular set of components; select a different tab to see a different set of components. Since first introduced, the JTabbedPane allowed you to place text and an icon on each tab, but people weren't happy with only text and icons. A little more functionality has been completed with the Java 6 release: components directly placed on tabs, as demonstrated in Figure 4-23.

To set the title of a tab, you specify the title text and which tab you are configuring. Setting up a tab to be used with a Component is done similarly with the setTabComponentAt() method, which passes in the tab index and component object to be used.

```
Component comp = ...;
JTabbedPane pane = new JTabbedPane();
pane.setTabComponentAt(0, comp);
```

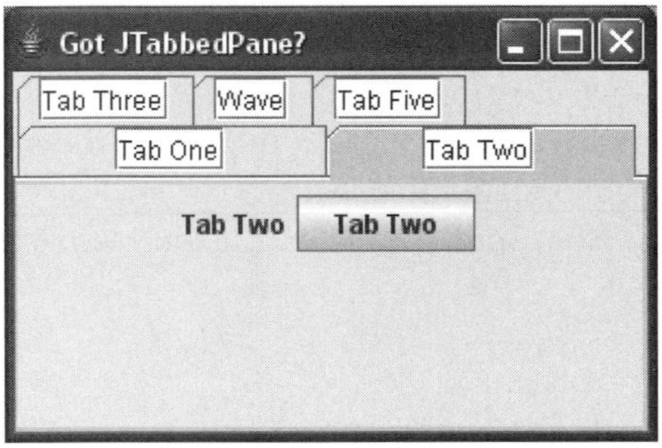

Figure 4-23. *A JTabbedPane with component tabs*

Basically, you have three methods to play with: setTabComponentAt(int index, Component comp), getTabComponentAt(int index), and indexOfTabComponent(Component). The last one tries to locate a placed component for you.

Listing 4-10 demonstrates the usage of this new API. As the API dictates, you can technically use either Swing or AWT components. However, I wouldn't recommend mixing the two. In this particular example, a JTextField is used as the label for each tab. It is editable, so if you don't like the default name of a tab, you can rename it.

Listing 4-10. *Components on a JTabbedPane*

```java
import java.awt.*;
import javax.swing.*;

public class TabSample {
  static void addIt(JTabbedPane tabbedPane, String text) {
    JLabel label = new JLabel(text);
    JButton button = new JButton(text);
    JPanel panel = new JPanel();
    panel.add(label);
    panel.add(button);
    tabbedPane.addTab(text, panel);
    tabbedPane.setTabComponentAt(tabbedPane.getTabCount()-1,
      new JTextField(text));
  }
  public static void main(String args[]) {
    Runnable runner = new Runnable() {
      public void run() {
        JFrame f = new JFrame("Got JTabbedPane?");
        f.setDefaultCloseOperation(JFrame.EXIT_ON_CLOSE);
        JTabbedPane tabbedPane = new JTabbedPane();
        addIt(tabbedPane, "Tab One");
        addIt(tabbedPane, "Tab Two");
        addIt(tabbedPane, "Tab Three");
        addIt(tabbedPane, "Tab Four");
        addIt(tabbedPane, "Tab Five");
        f.add(tabbedPane, BorderLayout.CENTER);
        f.setSize(300, 200);
        f.setVisible(true);
      }
    };
    EventQueue.invokeLater(runner);
  }
}
```

Text Component Printing

In the same manner that J2SE 5.0 simplified printing of JTable components, Java 6 simplifies the printing of the different JTextComponent subclasses, like JTextField, JTextArea, and JTextPane, to name a few. While you could always print the text components before, you were responsible for pagination and the like. Now, it's all done for you—you just need to call one of the new `print()` methods, of which there are three.

The simplest way to print the contents of a text component is to call its no-argument `print()` method. Figure 4-24 shows what the initial program looks like, and Figure 4-25 shows the standard printer dialog. The program in Listing 4-11 simply shows a `JTextArea`, pastes the current clipboard contents into it, and offers a Print button for printing the content.

Figure 4-24. *Printing the contents of a text component*

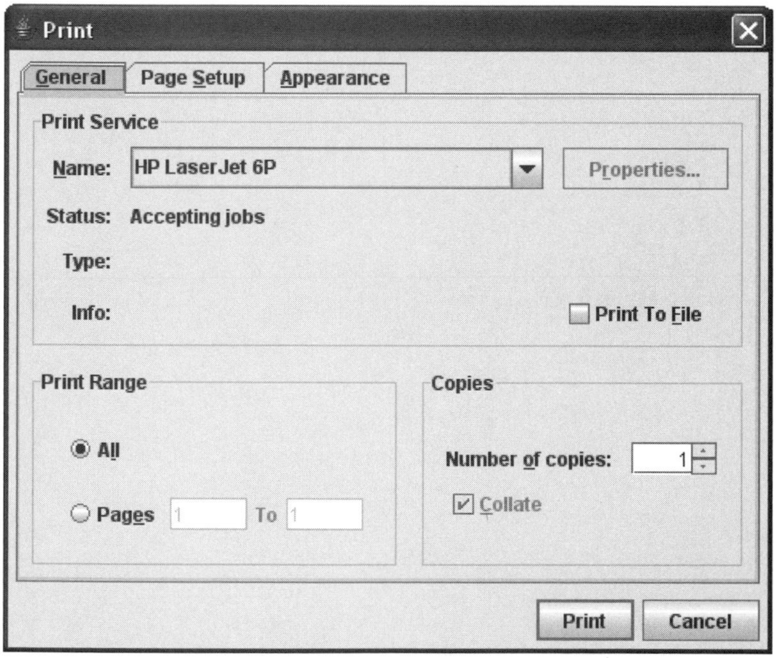

Figure 4-25. *The printer dialog*

Listing 4-11. *Printing Text Components*

```java
import javax.swing.*;
import java.awt.*;
import java.awt.event.*;
import java.awt.print.*;

public class TextPrint {
  public static void main(final String args[]) {
    Runnable runner = new Runnable() {
      public void run() {
        JFrame frame = new JFrame("Text Print");
        frame.setDefaultCloseOperation(JFrame.EXIT_ON_CLOSE);

        final JTextArea textArea = new JTextArea();
        JScrollPane pane = new JScrollPane(textArea);
        frame.add(pane, BorderLayout.CENTER);
        textArea.paste();

        JButton button = new JButton("Print");
        frame.add(button, BorderLayout.SOUTH);
        ActionListener listener = new ActionListener() {
          public void actionPerformed(ActionEvent e) {
            try {
              textArea.print();
            } catch (PrinterException pe) {
              System.err.println("Unable to print...");
            }
          }
        };
        button.addActionListener(listener);

        frame.setSize(250, 150);
        frame.setVisible(true);
      }
    };
    EventQueue.invokeLater(runner);
  }
}
```

The print() method is itself kind of generic. While it does offer you the interactive printer-selection dialog, you don't get a footer or header on each page. In order to do this, you need to use the second variety of the method: print(MessageFormat header, MessageFormat footer).

The most interesting of all the print() methods is the full-featured one:

```
public boolean print(MessageFormat headerFormat,
  MessageFormat footerFormat,
  boolean showPrintDialog,
  PrintService service,
  PrintRequestAttributeSet attributes,
  boolean interactive)
```

This last version lets you decide on more configuration options, like the inclusion or exclusion of the printer dialog, and the initial set of printer attributes. This version is the most flexible, and is what the other two varieties actually call to do their work.

■**Note** All three print() methods of JTextComponent will block until the print job is queued. If you want this queuing operation to happen in the background, you'll need to fork off another thread.

Drag-and-Drop Support

After cleaning up my desktop machine, I discovered that I've been writing about drag-and-drop support in Java since May 12, 1998. With Mustang, drag-and-drop support has undergone another significant set of changes—for the better, it looks like. There are two enhancements in this area with Mustang:

- Customizable drop modes that don't have to use selection to indicate drop location.

- Additional information is now available during transferable operations. This added information provides sufficient context to make a more informed decision about whether or not you should be able to perform a drop operation, like location-sensitive drop targets.

First off are the customizable drop modes. JList, JTable, JTextComponent, and JTree have a new setDropMode() method, which accepts a DropMode argument. Each particular component has a specific set of drop modes that it considers acceptable.

All components support a drop mode of USE_SELECTION; this is the historical way of indicating where to drop something. For instance, a text component will move the caret to indicate drop position. This is the default drop mode setting. The remaining options do *not* have an effect on component selection.

A DropMode of ON is supported by JList, JTable, and JTree. It allows you to drop objects on top of other items. This is useful for such tasks as dropping a file on a trash can to delete it, or on a JTree node to create a subtree. A drop mode of INSERT works for all four component types and allows you to drop items between other items, like between nodes of a tree or elements of a list. The ON_OR_INSERT mode goes back to the first three, JList, JTable, and JTree, and supports either mode of operation.

The JTable component has four additional drop mode options: INSERT_COLS, INSERT_ROWS, ON_OR_INSERT_COLS, and ON_OR_INSERT_ROWS. These restrict dropping over a JTable to one-directional changes if desired.

To demonstrate the different drop mode options, Figure 4-26 shows the program's window. It provides a draggable JTextField at the top, a droppable JTree in the middle, and a JComboBox at the bottom for selection of drop mode options.

Basically, you can type something in the JTextField, highlight it, and drag it over the JTree. You can then drop the text and see the different behaviors for the different drop mode settings. Figure 4-27 shows the USE_SELECTION behavior. As you move the mouse over the tree, you lose any indication of selection prior to the drop initiation. Figure 4-28 shows the ON behavior. Here, you see both the previously selected item and the current drop location. The INSERT drop mode is shown in Figure 4-29. When dragging an object above a tree with the drop mode set to INSERT, you get a narrow line that appears between two nodes of the tree. When the drop mode is set to ON_OR_INSERT, the tree acts like a combination of ON and INSERT, and doesn't require its own screen dump, as the drop indicator depends upon the position of the mouse and alternates between the two options based on position.

Figure 4-26. *A JTree with support for dropping items*

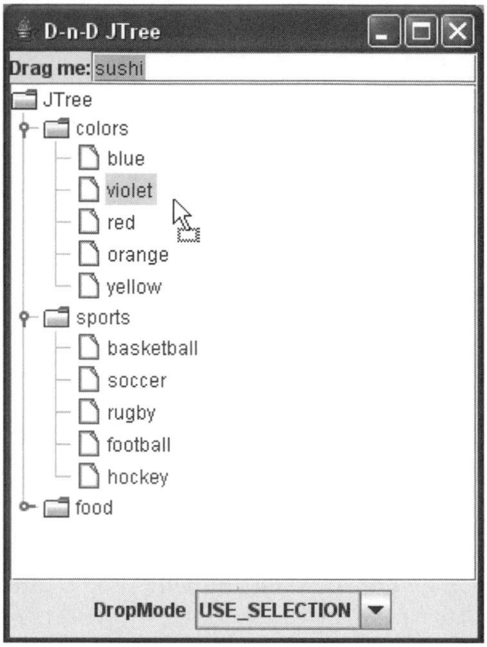

Figure 4-27. *USE_SELECTION drop mode*

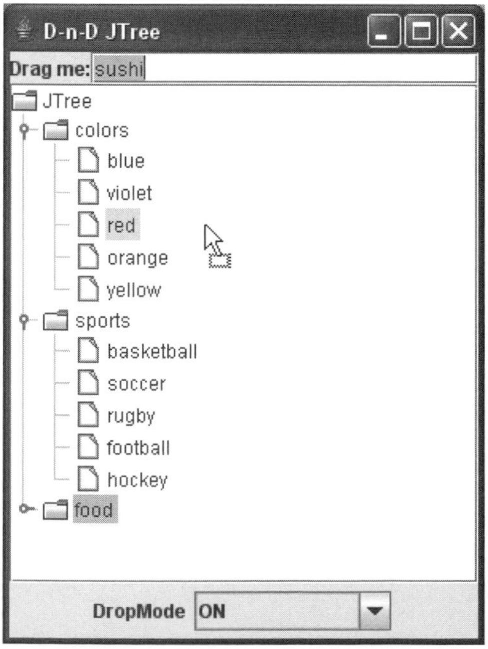

Figure 4-28. *ON drop mode*

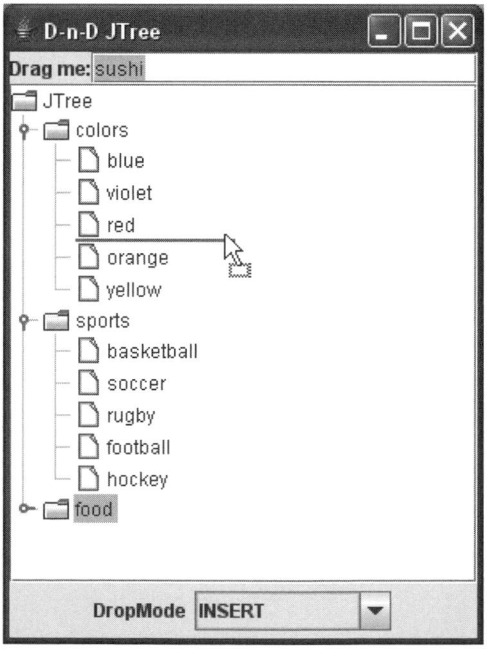

Figure 4-29. *INSERT drop mode*

While Java 5 added built-in drag-and-drop support for several components, it didn't define drop behavior for a JTree. Java 6 doesn't help there, either. If you want to be able to drop items on a JTree, you have to do it yourself. The way to do this is to define a TransferHandler and associate it with the JTree. TransferHandler has many methods, but thankfully you don't have to override many to create a handler for a JTree—in fact, only two: public boolean canImport(TransferHandler.TransferSupport support) and public boolean importData(TransferHandler.TransferSupport support).

The canImport() method of TransferHandler lets you define when, where, and what you can import. The method returns a boolean, where true indicates that it is OK to transfer and false indicates that it is not. To keep things simple in the following code snippet, only strings will be transferable and only drop operations will be supported. The cut-and-paste operation will not be supported, even though it uses the same mechanism. Lastly, if the tree path is empty, that too is a failure case.

```
public boolean canImport(TransferHandler.TransferSupport support) {
  if (!support.isDataFlavorSupported(DataFlavor.stringFlavor) ||
      !support.isDrop()) {
    return false;
  }

  JTree.DropLocation dropLocation =
    (JTree.DropLocation)support.getDropLocation();

  return dropLocation.getPath() != null;
}
```

The importData() method is a little more complicated. Essentially, you have to get the data, find the right place in the TreePath for the insertion, create the node, insert it, and, to be nice, make sure that the newly inserted node is visible. Listing 4-12 includes the importData() definition, along with the complete source used to generate Figure 4-26.

Listing 4-12. *Demonstrating Drop Modes with a JTree*

```
import java.awt.*;
import java.awt.datatransfer.*;
import java.awt.event.*;
import java.io.*;
import javax.swing.*;
import javax.swing.tree.*;
```

```java
public class DndTree {
  public static void main(String args[]) {
    Runnable runner = new Runnable() {
      public void run() {
        JFrame f = new JFrame("D-n-D JTree");
        f.setDefaultCloseOperation(JFrame.EXIT_ON_CLOSE);

        JPanel top = new JPanel(new BorderLayout());
        JLabel dragLabel = new JLabel("Drag me:");
        JTextField text = new JTextField();
        text.setDragEnabled(true);
        top.add(dragLabel, BorderLayout.WEST);
        top.add(text, BorderLayout.CENTER);
        f.add(top, BorderLayout.NORTH);

        final JTree tree = new JTree();
        final DefaultTreeModel model = (DefaultTreeModel)tree.getModel();
        tree.setTransferHandler(new TransferHandler() {
          /**
            * Returns true if flavor of data is string, operation is
            * a drop operation, and path is non-null.
            */
          public boolean canImport(TransferHandler.TransferSupport support) {
            if (!support.isDataFlavorSupported(DataFlavor.stringFlavor) ||
                !support.isDrop()) {
              return false;
            }

            JTree.DropLocation dropLocation =
              (JTree.DropLocation)support.getDropLocation();

            return dropLocation.getPath() != null;
          }

          /**
            * Performs actual import operation. Returns true on success
            * and false otherwise.
            */
          public boolean importData(TransferHandler.TransferSupport support) {
            if (!canImport(support)) {
              return false;
            }
```

```java
  // Fetch the drop location
JTree.DropLocation dropLocation =
  (JTree.DropLocation)support.getDropLocation();

  // Fetch the tree path
TreePath path = dropLocation.getPath();

  // Fetch the transferable object
Transferable transferable = support.getTransferable();

  // Fetch the transfer data in the proper format
  // from the transferable object
String transferData;
try {
  transferData = (String)transferable.getTransferData(
    DataFlavor.stringFlavor);
} catch (IOException e) {
  return false;
} catch (UnsupportedFlavorException e) {
  return false;
}

  // Fetch the drop location
int childIndex = dropLocation.getChildIndex();
// -1 means drop location is parent node, which is translated to end
if (childIndex == -1) {
  childIndex = model.getChildCount(path.getLastPathComponent());
}

// Create new node
DefaultMutableTreeNode newNode =
  new DefaultMutableTreeNode(transferData);
// Insert new node at proper location
DefaultMutableTreeNode parentNode =
  (DefaultMutableTreeNode)path.getLastPathComponent();
model.insertNodeInto(newNode, parentNode, childIndex);

// Make new node visible
TreePath newPath = path.pathByAddingChild(newNode);
tree.makeVisible(newPath);
tree.scrollRectToVisible(tree.getPathBounds(newPath));
```

```
              return true;
          }
      });

      JScrollPane pane = new JScrollPane(tree);
      f.add(pane, BorderLayout.CENTER);

      JPanel bottom = new JPanel();
      JLabel comboLabel = new JLabel("DropMode");
      String options[] = {"USE_SELECTION",
              "ON", "INSERT", "ON_OR_INSERT"
      };
      final DropMode mode[] = {DropMode.USE_SELECTION,
              DropMode.ON, DropMode.INSERT, DropMode.ON_OR_INSERT};
      final JComboBox combo = new JComboBox(options);
      combo.addActionListener(new ActionListener() {
        public void actionPerformed(ActionEvent e) {
          int selectedIndex = combo.getSelectedIndex();
          tree.setDropMode(mode[selectedIndex]);
        }
      });
      bottom.add(comboLabel);
      bottom.add(combo);
      f.add(bottom, BorderLayout.SOUTH);
      f.setSize(300, 400);
      f.setVisible(true);
    }
  };
  EventQueue.invokeLater(runner);
 }
}
```

■Note You can override the public boolean shouldIndicate(TransferHandler.TransferSupport support, boolean canImport) method of TransferHandler to say whether the drop location should be indicated when over a potential drop target. This is different than performing location-sensitive drop operations, which would involve getting the drop location from the TransferSupport object passed to the canImport() method, and performing some check based on that location.

The second half to the new drag-and-drop support in Java 6 is actually demonstrated in this example. It is the `TransferHandler.TransferSupport` object passed into the `importData()` method. It defines several properties that you can use when deciding whether to allow data importing. These properties are as follows:

- *Component*: The target component of the transfer

- *Data flavors*: The supported data formats available

- *Drop actions*: The action being performed, the source drop actions, and the user drop action

- *Drop location*: The possible location of a drop, or null if not a drop operation

- *Transferable*: The actual `Transferable` object

- *Drop*: The current operation type (drop, as opposed to cut and paste)

In addition to these properties of `TransferSupport`, there is a method for checking whether the `TransferHandler` supports the flavor: `isDataFlavorSupported(DataFlavor)`. It no longer is necessary to loop through all available flavors to see if there is a match. This inner class of `TransferHandler` should allow developers to enable more informed decision-making when designing drop zones for data transfers.

More Miscellaneous Stuff

The Swing packages had more "big" idea changes than little additions here and there. Some smaller-scale changes include the addition of `Cursor` support to `JInternalFrame` objects, the addition of fields that can be associated with an `Action`, and the addition of `TableStringConverter`, a helper class that lets you convert `TableModel` cells to an appropriate string representation. There is even a new `FileNameExtensionFilter` for working with the `JFileChooser`.

Summary

This chapter has introduced some of the more visual items added to the latest desktop Java release. You learned about having fun with splash screens and the system tray. You explored the new modality options for pop-up windows, and discovered that you can now write GIF images without the risk of patent violations. Also on the AWT front were the latest antialiasing enhancements. In the Swing world, you explored the sorting and filtering enhancements to the JTable component, how the SwingWorker class was finally introduced to the standard platform libraries, and how to place components on tabs of a JTabbedPane. Printing text components is another feature added to Mustang, along with another round of improvements to drag-and-drop support.

The next chapter takes you to the latest improvements to JDBC (the trademarked name that is not an acronym for Java Database Connectivity). You'll see how the 4.0 version of the API to access SQL data stores makes life even easier for you.

CHAPTER 5

■■■

JDBC 4.0

Need to access a database? Since the original JDBC API was added to JDK 1.1, the JDBC API has offered support for connecting your Java programs to SQL-based data sources. And, while JDBC is not an acronym for Java Database Connectivity (at least according to Sun), what you may be tired of doing with JDBC is loading database drivers. One of the many new features added to Mustang is the ability to access JDBC connections without having to explicitly load the driver, provided it is packaged properly. As Tables 5-1 and 5-2 show, the java.sql package has grown quite a bit, while javax.sql and its subpackages have barely grown at all.

Table 5-1. *java.sql.* Package Sizes*

Package	Version	Interfaces	Classes	Enums	Throwable	Annotations	Total
sql	5.0	18	7	0	0+4	0	29
sql	6.0	27	8	3	0+19	4	61
Delta		9	1	3	0+15	4	32

Table 5-2. *javax.sql.* Package Sizes*

Package	Version	Interfaces	Classes	Throwable	Total
sql	5.0	12	2	0+0	14
sql	6.0	14	3	0+0	17
sql.rowset	5.0	7	2	0+1	10
sql.rowset	6.0	7	2	0+1	10
sql.rowset.serial	5.0	0	9	0+1	10
sql.rowset.serial	6.0	0	9	0+1	10
sql.rowset.spi	5.0	4	2	0+2	8
sql.rowset.spi	6.0	4	2	0+2	8
Delta		2	1	0+0	3

There are many different areas to explore what's new and different with JDBC 4.0. In addition to the new driver-loading capabilities, you'll discover many other features added to Mustang via JSR 221, many times to add support for new SQL 2003 features. According to the original Java Specification Request, one of the primary goals of the new release is ease of use. You be the judge on how well Sun did.

■**Note** The examples in this chapter are purposely just code snippets, not complete programs. This was done to avoid spending too much time in setup of your system and identifying whether all the features are supported with your installed database selection, in favor of actually learning what's new and different with Java 6.

The java.sql and javax.sql Packages

The java.sql package is the primary package for JDBC. It offers the main classes for interacting with your data sources. Since the changes to javax.sql are so small, I'll cover the two together. The new features in these packages for Mustang include changes in the following areas:

- Database driver loading

- Exception handling improvements

- Enhanced BLOB/CLOB functionality

- Connection and statement interface enhancements

- National character set support

- SQL ROWID access

- SQL 2003 XML data type support

- Annotations

Database Driver Loading

Mustang changes the requirement that you must explicitly load/register the database driver that your JDBC program needs. Since Chapter 1, there have been several examples of using the new service provider interface introduced with Mustang. Create a subdirectory named services under the META-INF directory for your JAR file and place an appropriately named text file in the directory for the service provider to be discovered, and the Java runtime environment will locate it when requested (specifics to be shown shortly). This is exactly how the new support for loading JDBC drivers has been added to Mustang. Provided the vendor for your JDBC driver packages up the driver in this new way, you don't have to explicitly load the driver yourself.

Before Mustang, the way to load the JDBC driver wasn't difficult; it just required you to learn what the right class name was for the driver from a particular vendor.

```
Class.forName("oracle.jdbc.driver.OracleDriver");
// or DriverManager.registerDriver(new oracle.jdbc.driver.OracleDriver());
Connection con = DriverManager.getConnection(url, username, password);
```

Now, you can drop that first line there, and essentially just use the driver directly.

```
Connection con = DriverManager.getConnection(url, username, password);
```

One question comes up frequently when people hear about this new feature: what happens when multiple drivers installed as services are available for the same database connection type? It works in CLASSPATH order. The first JAR file with a matching connection from the DriverManager will be used. This is really no different than before if you called Class.forName(), passing in a driver name found in multiple JAR files.

What happened to creating connections using a DataSource? It still works, though it isn't necessary in stand-alone applications. According to a blog entry from Amit Handa of Sun (http://blogs.sun.com/roller/page/blogAmit?entry=jdbc_driver_loading_with_mustang), "Nothing changes in the Java EE world. This driver loading is primarily for non managed scenarios or stand alone applications. The way you get a connection from a DataSource stays as it is."

If you are interested in doing this for your own JDBC driver, place the name of the java.sql.Driver implementation class in the file META-INF/services/java.sql.Driver.

```
> cat META-INF/services/java.sql.Driver
net.zukowski.revealed.sql.MyDriver
```

Exception Handling Improvements

There are three areas in which exception handling for your JDBC code has improved with the changes in JDBC 4.0. First off, you can use the Java 5 enhanced for loop to easily iterate through the cause of an exception. Secondly, there are new constructors for SQLException to pass in the underlying reason for the SQLException. And, lastly, there are many new subclasses of SQLException for cleaner handling of exceptions with their own catch clauses.

In order to support the enhanced `for` loop, the `SQLException` class now implements the `Iterable<T>` interface, where `T` is `Throwable`. The internal vector of `SQLException` objects can be looped through easily in the `catch` clause of your JDBC code.

```
try {
...
} catch (SQLException sqle) {
  for(Throwable t : sqle) {
    System.out.println("Throwable: " + t);
  }
}
```

Not only does the class implement `Iterable`, but there are four new constructors for `SQLException`, passing in the cause of the underlying SQL exception:

- `SQLException(Throwable cause)`

- `SQLException(String reason, Throwable cause)`

- `SQLException(String reason, String sqlState, Throwable cause)`

- `SQLException(String reason, String sqlState, int vendorCode, Throwable cause)`

This allows you to discover that, say, an `IOException` caused the `SQLException`. This changes the earlier code snippet a little bit to check for causes, and not just loop through all the SQL exceptions.

```
try {
...
} catch (SQLException sqle) {
  for(Throwable t : sqle) {
    System.out.println("Throwable: " + t);
    Throwable cause = t.getCause();
    while (cause != null) {
      System.out.println("Cause: " + cause);
      cause = cause.getCause();
    }
  }
}
```

The last set of exceptional changes are the new subclasses of `SQLException`, which allow you to handle each type differently and with ease in its own `catch` clause, without having to try to figure out what really went wrong based on associated error codes.

Since the beginning of JDBC time, the `SQLException` class has had a `getSQLState()` method to get the associated SQL state string for the exception, and a vendor-specific error code, accessible from the getErrorCode() method. These methods are still there and can be used; but in addition to these methods, there are now subclasses specific to common SQL states. There are also two new categories for SQL exceptions: transient and nontransient. These are represented by the new SQLTransientException and SQLNonTransientException classes.

Transient exceptions are those that when retried could succeed without changing anything. These exceptions include the following subclasses:

- SQLTimeoutException: Expired statement timeout

- SQLTransactionRollbackException: Database rolled back statement automatically, possibly due to deadlock (SQLState 40)

- SQLTransientConnectionException: Communication layer problem (SQLState 08)

Nontransient exceptions are those that will fail again on retry until the underlying cause of the problem is corrected. There are six subclasses of SQLNonTransientException:

- SQLDataException: Data error, such as an invalid argument (SQLState 22)

- SQLFeatureNotSupportedException: JDBC driver doesn't support feature (SQLState 0A)

- SQLIntegrityConstraintViolationException: Constraint on a key was violated (SQLState 23)

- SQLInvalidAuthorizationSpecException: Invalid authorization credentials presented during connection (SQLState 28)

- SQLNonTransientConnectionException: Communication layer problem that cannot be corrected (SQLState 08)

- SQLSyntaxErrorException: Query violated SQL syntax (SQLState 42)

In some cases, such as SQLFeatureNotSupportedException, the fix for the problem is to get a new database driver, not to necessarily change anything in code. The connection exception can be transient or nontransient, depending upon what the problem is—hence the shared SQLState value of 08.

Enhanced BLOB/CLOB Functionality

BLOBs and CLOBs can be fun. They represent binary and character large objects stored in the database system. Prior to JDBC 4.0, there were some areas of the API that could lead to some ambiguity. Changes in Mustang fix these. For instance, instead of having to call setCharacterStream(int parameterIndex, Reader reader, int length) on a PreparedStatement and letting the system possibly incorrectly determine whether the column was a LONGVARCHAR or a CLOB, you can now explicitly call setClob(int parameterIndex, Reader reader, long length). Other changes include the following methods for creating empty objects in the Connection interface: createBlob(), createClob(), and createNClob(). In addition, methods were added to the Blob/Clob interfaces for freeing the object and fetching pieces of it. Lastly, we can't forget the new NClob interface. This works like the Blob and Clob interfaces when working with result sets, callable statements, and prepared statements.

Connection and Statement Interface Enhancements

The Connection and Statement interfaces are important in the world of JDBC. For Connection, an instance of the interface still describes a database session. Statement is still a SQL statement to get a ResultSet. You can now do just a little bit more with both.

The Connection interface has two significant changes, covered by five methods. The first change has to do with checking whether a connection hasn't been closed and is still valid. You can now do that with the new isValid() method.

```
public boolean isValid(int timeout)
```

The timeout here represents the number of seconds to wait for a reply. If no reply is acquired during this time, false is returned and the caller is unblocked. A timeout value of 0 means it will wait forever.

The other new feature of Connection is the ability to query for and set the connection's client info properties. This is a Properties object and works much the same as the System class does with system properties. The getter methods return all the properties, or that for one particular name.

- public Properties getClientInfo()

- public String getClientInfo(String name)

The setter methods go in the opposite direction. The first version allows you to set multiple name/value pairs simultaneously.

- public void setClientInfo(Properties props)

- public void setClientInfo(String name, String value)

That isn't quite it yet for client info properties. You can actually ask the DatabaseMetaData for the set of properties supported, via its getClientInfoProperties() method. This method returns a sorted ResultSet by name, not just a list of names. For each property, you can get its name, maximum length, default value, and a description of the property.

While the `Statement` object has a new `isClosed()` method to indicate whether a statement is closed, the more important changes have to do with the `PreparedStatement` interface. Two new methods are `isPoolable()` and `setPoolable()`. You can now request a `PreparedStatement` to either be pooled or not. Pooled statements can be shared by the statement pool manager across multiple connections. The request is just a hint, though, and may be ignored.

Over on the `javax.sql` side, you'll find the `PooledConnection` interface. This now allows you to register a `StatementEventListener` with the connection. Any registered listeners of the connection would then be notified when a prepared statement is closed or has become invalid. The listener notification includes a `StatementEvent`, which includes the `SQLException` that is about to be thrown and the `PreparedStatement` that is being closed or is invalid.

National Character Set Support

National character set types are new to SQL 2003. They offer direct support in the database of a character set that is different than the database character set. They allow you to mix content—such as a variable-width multibyte character set with one that is fixed-width, for instance. JDBC 4.0 adds support for these new set types: NCHAR, NVARCHAR, LONGNVARCHAR, and NCLOB, where the *N* here represents the national character set version of the data type without the *N*. The NCHAR, NVARCHAR, and LONGNVARCHAR types are automatically converted to the Java runtime's character set, and back, as needed. NCLOB does not support an automatic conversion between CLOB and NCLOB.

Existing core interfaces have been modified to deal with the new national character set support. It has been added to the `PreparedStatement` and `CallableStatement` interfaces through their new `setNString()`, `setNCharacterStream()`, and `setNClob()` methods. In addition, the `ResultSet` interface has new `getNString()`, `getNCharacterStream()`, and `getNClob()` methods, along with `updateNString()`, `updateNCharacterStream()`, and `updateNClob()` methods.

To demonstrate, the following query fetches two columns from a table, one involving the national character set, and the other not:

```
Console console = System.console();
String nString = ...;
String query = "select ncol, name from students where ncol=?";
PreparedStatement pstmt = con.prepareStatement(query);
pstmt.setNString(1, nString);
ResultSet rs = pstmt.executeQuery();
while(rs.next) {
  console.printf("ncol= %s, name=%s%n", rs.getNString(1), rs.getString(2));
}
```

SQL ROWID Access

Yet another interesting feature of JDBC 4.0 is support for accessing the SQL built-in type ROWID, for uniquely identifying the table row. One key thing to mention here: it is only available if the underlying database supports giving it to you. To find this out, you must ask `DatabaseMetaData`. Its `getRowIdLifetime()` method returns a `RowIdLifetime`, which has an enumeration of possible values:

- ROWID_UNSUPPORTED

- ROWID_VALID_FOREVER

- ROWID_VALID_SESSION

- ROWID_VALID_TRANSACTION

- ROWID_VALID_OTHER

Most of the values are fairly self-explanatory. `ROWID_UNSUPPORTED` means the data source doesn't support the feature. `ROWID_VALID_FOREVER` is, like a diamond, forever. `ROWID_VALID_SESSION` means for at least the session, while `ROWID_VALID_TRANSACTION` means for the transaction. `ROWID_VALID_OTHER` means you can get a row ID from the system but have no clue how long it will last. Effectively, you should treat this as `ROWID_UNSUPPORTED`, as it can go away at any time.

If the data sources returns a `RowId`, you can get its value as either bytes via `getBytes()` or as a `String` with `toString()`. Which of the two you work with depends on your needs. Of course, sometimes just `RowId` is sufficient. Here's a simple look at its usage:

```
ResultSet rs = stmt.executeQuery("select name, rank, ROWID from people");
while (rs.next()) {
  String name = getString(1);
  String rank = getString(2);
  RowId rowid = getRowId(3);

  ...
}
```

SQL 2003 XML Data Type Support

Another big feature added to SQL 2003 is support for XML as a native data type in the database. From your Java programs, you no longer have to use CLOBs to access the XML data elements. You get a JDBC 4.0 mapping direct to the SQL XML type with Mustang.

When querying a database with an XML column, the type returned from the result set is of type SQLXML. While Chapter 6 looks more at the updated XML support in Mustang, we'll look at the database side more here; not actually reading/writing the contents, just fetching.

The SQLXML interface is rather small, with just nine methods:

- public void free()

- public InputStream getBinaryStream()

- public Reader getCharacterStream()

- public <T extends Source> T getSource(Class<T> sourceClass)

- public String getString()

- public OutputStream setBinaryStream()

- public Writer setCharacterStream()

- public <T extends Result> T setResult(Class<T> resultClass)

- public void setString(String value)

Working with the String representation is relatively easy. The StAX stream representation of the XML value is the more interesting bit (it's saved for a later chapter). StAX is the Streaming API for XML added with JSR 173. Here's what a simple retrieval loop might look like:

```
ResultSet rs = ...;
while (rs.next()) {
  SQLXML xmlField = st.getSQLXML("xml_field");
  String string = xmlField.getString()
  xmlField.free();
}
```

The loop gets more interesting and involved once you work with the XMLStreamWriter.

Creation of data for an XML column is a little more involved than for non-XML columns. You must create the SQLXML item first, fill it, and then associate it with the statement. Not complicated, but it really depends upon what you do with the XMLStreamWriter.

```
// Assuming you have a table with an integer column and an XML column
String sql ="insert into blogTable (userid, blog) values (?, ?)";
PreparedStatement prep =connection.prepareStatement(sql);
int userId = 12345;
prepStmt.setInt(1, userId);
SQLXML blogvalue = connection.createSQLXML();
Writer writer = blogvalue.setCharacterStream();
// write to stream, code not supplied
...
writer.close();
prepStmt.setSQLXML(2, blogvalue);
int rowCount = prepStmt.executeUpdate();
```

Another aspect of the XML support available with Mustang includes the SQL syntax changes when making SQL/XML queries. Through careful use of the new xmlelement() SQL function, the results you get back from non-XML-based data sources can be well-formed XML documents. For instance, here's an SQL query that generates a well-formed XML document for each row of a result set, where the outermost tag is user and the two columns are id and name:

```
select xmlelement(name "user", xmlelement(name "id", p.userid),
  xmlelement(name "name", p.username)) from passwords p
```

Tip For more information on XML support within SQL 2003, see the SQL/XML tutorial at www.stylusstudio.com/sqlxml_tutorial.html.

Annotations

While Chapter 10 covers the new annotation support found in Java 6, some annotations are specific to JDBC, and so are covered here. There happen to be four new JDBC-related annotations added to Java 6.0: Select, Update, ResultColumn, and AutoGeneratedKeys.

Note If you aren't familiar with annotations, you might want to read up on this Java 5 feature before reading more of this section. Chapter 10 will cover annotations in more depth—but hey, this book is about Java 6, not Java 5.

The annotations found in the java.sql package are meant to simplify object-relational mappings. They allow you to place an annotated SQL statement in code, flagging it with an annotation so you know what type of statement it is, and thus what it can return.

To demonstrate, you need to define a class to represent the DataSet to work with. In this particular case, it's a simple student definition that maps to a database table. DataSet is itself an interface of the java.sql package that you'll see used shortly.

```
public class Student {
  public int id;
  public String first;
  public String last;
}
```

In your class definition, if the columns don't match the database column names exactly, you'll need to use the @Select annotation to connect the mismatched columns— as in public @ResultColumn("last") String lastName; if the database column name is last but you want to access it in the Student class as lastName. Here is an interface to query for all the students and delete them all:

```
interface MyQueries extends BaseQuery {
    @Select("select id, first, last from students")
    DataSet<Student> getAllStudents();

    @Update("delete * from students")
    int deleteAllStudents();
}
```

The BaseQuery interface of the java.sql package is needed for all queries. Just extend it with the annotated SQL operations you plan on performing. The @Select annotation returns a DataSet—not a ResultSet—while @Update returns a count. The DataSet interface extends the List interface from the collections framework, so you can use the results of the getAllStudents() call in an enhanced for loop. For instance, here's some sample code that deletes any student name of John:

```
MyQueries mq = con.createQueryObject(MyQueries.class);
DataSet rows = mq.getAllStudents();

for (Student student: rows) {
  if (student.firstName.equals("John")) {
    rows.delete();
  }
}
```

The parameterized DataSet allows you to manipulate the results of your query. Insertion is done by creating a new element and calling the insert() method of the returned DataSet. Updates are done with the modify() method. Disconnected data sets can be synchronized back to the underlying data store using the sync() method.

Summary

JDBC 4.0 adds many interesting new features to the database world. Ease of use has definitely come to the forefront with the latest changes. While database driver loading is one less thing you need to do with Mustang, the other changes add to what you can do with JDBC. Enhancements seem to be everywhere—from the improvements to exception handling and BLOBs, to CLOBs, connections, and statements. You can get notification of new statement events, and you can check for connection closure now where you couldn't before. Most of the rest of the changes involve the addition of SQL 2003–related support to the Java platform, with its new national character set support, SQL ROWID access, and the very popular XML data type support. Also, the new annotations available with JDBC 4.0 can greatly simplify your life.

As promised, in the next chapter you'll jump into the updates to the XML world of Java 6. Added with JSR 173, you'll learn about the Streaming API for XML; with JSR 222, you'll take a look at JAXB 2.0 support; and with JSR 105, you'll learn about the new API supporting XML digital signatures.

■**Note** As this book went to press, the build 88 drop of Mustang came out. One big addition included with this release is the open source Apache Derby project (http://db.apache.org/derby). This is a 100-percent Java database shipping with the runtime. Sun's distribution of Derby is called Java DB. You can read more about the project at http://developers.sun.com/prodtech/javadb. The inclusion of the database with the runtime offers a lightweight database solution.

CHAPTER 6

■ ■ ■

Extensible Markup Language (XML)

What's new with Extensible Markup Language (XML)? As XML seems to evolve on a separate path from the Java platform, each new release of the Java Standard Edition brings the latest versions of the different parts of the XML stack into the mainline. Typically, these have evolved through their own JSR process or standard outside the Java Community Process (JCP); and releases like Merlin, Tiger, and now Mustang just bless the latest release of some XML piece for their individual release. With Mustang, three pieces to the XML puzzle are added: the Java Architecture for XML Binding (JAXB) 2.0, XML digital signatures, and the Streaming API for XML.

Looking at the packages related to XML in Java 6, it is a little difficult to present what's new and different in table form. The JAXB libraries are new, and are found in `javax.xml.bind` and its subpackages. The XML digital signature libraries are new, and found in `javax.xml.crypto` and its subpackages, and the libraries for the Streaming API for XML are found in `javax.xml.stream` and its subpackages. You even get a new `javax.xml.soap` package for classes to help you build up SOAP messages—but more on that in Chapter 7, in which I'll discuss the new `javax.xml.ws` package and subpackages for the web services APIs. For those packages that exist in both Java 5 and 6, Table 6-1 shows off their single difference: yet another new package for the Streaming API for XML, `javax.xml.transform.stax`.

Table 6-1. *javax.xml.* Package Sizes*

Package	Version	Interfaces	Classes	Throwable	Total
xml	5.0	0	1	0+0	1
xml	6.0	0	1	0+0	1
xml.datatype	5.0	0	5	1+0	6
xml.datatype	6.0	0	5	1+0	6
xml.namespace	5.0	1	1	0+0	2
xml.namespace	6.0	1	1	0+0	2
xml.parsers	5.0	0	4	1+1	6
xml.parsers	6.0	0	4	1+1	6
xml.transform	5.0	6	3	2+1	12
xml.transform	6.0	6	3	2+1	12
xml.transform.dom	5.0	1	2	0+0	3
xml.transform.dom	6.0	1	2	0+0	3
xml.transform.sax	5.0	2	3	0+0	5
xml.transform.sax	6.0	2	3	0+0	5
xml.transform.stax	6.0	0	2	0+0	2
xml.transform.stream	5.0	0	2	0+0	2
xml.transform.stream	6.0	0	2	0+0	2
xml.validation	5.0	0	6	0+0	6
xml.validation	6.0	0	6	0+0	6
xml.xpath	5.0	5	2	4+0	11
xml.xpath	6.0	5	2	4+0	11
Delta		0	2	0+0	2

For all these packages, the bulk of the changes from 5.0 to 6.0 were related to documentation. The only code change outside of the javadoc comments was the addition of an overloaded newInstance() method for several factory classes: javax.xml.datatype. DatatypeFactory, javax.xml.parsers.DocumentBuilderFactory, javax.xml.parsers. SAXParserFactory, javax.xml.transform.TransformerFactory, and javax.xml.validation. SchemaFactory. While these classes had a newInstance() method already, the overloaded variety allows you to pass in the class loader to load the factory class, and not assume that the class loader for the context of the executing thread is appropriate.

The javax.xml.bind Package

JSR 31 defined the first release of the XML Data Binding Specification. According to its JSR description, its goal was to offer "a facility for compiling an XML Schema into one or more Java classes which can parse, generate, and validate documents that follow the schema." In overly simple terms, it lets you map JavaBeans components to XML documents, and vice versa. This was first made available as part of the Java Web Services Developer Pack (WSDP) and became standard fare for J2EE developers.

JSR 222 updates the original version of JAXB to the 2.0 release, and Mustang brings JAXB 2.0 into the Java 6 release with the javax.xml.bind package and its subpackages. In other words, as web services have become more mainstream and not limited to full-scale server-side applications, pieces of the web services pack, like JAXB, have joined the ranks of standard APIs in the desktop release of the Java platform. See Chapter 7 for more information on the web services support available with Mustang.

Many tutorials on JAXB 2.0 have been available online for some time for use with Java EE 5. With minimal changes, you can use these tutorials with Java SE 6. But, before jumping right into the how-to bit, it is important to point out what exactly JAXB 2.0 offers. Essentially, JAXB offers a mapping from a JavaBeans component to XML Schema, and vice versa. The 2.0 release of JAXB adds the Java-to-XML Schema support that wasn't found with 1.0. With 1.0, you can do XML Schema to Java, but not vice versa. Now, you can go both ways with JAXB 2.0.

Before digging too deeply into the details, it is important to show a quick example. Then I'll explain it, with more details of the API. Listing 6-1 defines an inner Point class whose state will be saved to an XML file. The important bit about the inner class is the @XmlRootElement annotation. As the name implies, the Point class will be used as an XML root element. Each JavaBeans property of the class will then become an element inside the root element.

Listing 6-1. *Using JAXB for Java-to-XML Generation*

```
import java.io.*;
import javax.xml.bind.*;
import javax.xml.bind.annotation.*;

public class J2S {

  public static void main(String[] args) {
    try {
      JAXBContext context = JAXBContext.newInstance(Point.class);
      Marshaller m = context.createMarshaller();
```

```
        m.setProperty(Marshaller.JAXB_FORMATTED_OUTPUT, true);
        Point p = new Point(3, 4);
        m.marshal(p, System.out);
      } catch (JAXBException jex) {
        System.out.println("JAXB Binding Exception");
        jex.printStackTrace();
      }
    }

    @XmlRootElement
    private static class Point {
      int x;
      int y;
      public Point() {
      }

      public Point(int x, int y) {
        this.x = x;
        this.y = y;
      }

      public void setX(int x) {
        this.x = x;
      }

      public void setY(int y) {
        this.y = y;
      }

      public int getX() {
        return x;
      }

      public int getY() {
        return y;
      }
    }
  }
```

Compile and run the program to see the following output:

```
> java J2S
<?xml version="1.0" encoding="UTF-8" standalone="yes"?>
<point>
    <x>3</x>
    <y>4</y>
</point>
```

As revealed by the generated XML, the newly defined Point class has two JavaBeans component properties: x and y. Their values were initialized to 3 and 4, respectively, before the Point was passed off to the Marshaller. It is the responsibility of the Marshaller to discover the necessary property names and values, and write them to the stream provided (System.out, in this case).

Note If the JAXB_FORMATTED_OUTPUT property in Listing 6-1 isn't set to true, all the output will be sent to a single line, without the benefit of new lines or spacing.

In addition to the @XmlRootElement annotation used in Listing 6-1, there are many other annotations found in the javax.xml.bind.annotation package. Table 6-2 lists them all, with brief descriptions of their purposes. Essentially, they all help to define how the JavaBeans components will be serialized and deserialized (or, in JAXB speak, *marshalled* and *unmarshalled*).

Table 6-2. *XML Schema Mapping Annotations*

Name	Description
XmlAccessorOrder	Controls ordering of fields and properties for a class
XmlAccessorType	Used in conjunction with the XmlAccessType Enum to indicate if a field or property should be serialized
XmlAnyAttribute	Acts as a map of wildcard attributes for java.util.Map properties or fields
XmlAnyElement	Serves to identify the catchall property during unmarshalling
XmlAttachmentRef	Used to identify mime types and URIs for external content
XmlAttribute	Allows renaming of a JavaBeans property to/from an XML attribute

Continued

Table 6-2. *Continued*

Name	Description
XmlElement	Allows mapping of a JavaBeans property to a complex type
XmlElementDecl	Works to map an object factory to an XML element
XmlElementRef	Works to map a JavaBeans property to an XML element derived from the property's type
XmlElementRefs	Marks a property that refers to classes with @XmlElement
XmlElements	Acts as a container for multiple @XmlElement annotations
XmlElementWrapper	Generates a wrapper element for XML representation
XmlEnum	Maps an Enum to an XML representation
XmlEnumValue	Identifies an enumerated constant
XmlID	Maps a property to an XML ID
XmlIDREF	Maps a property to an XML IDREF
XmlInlineBinaryData	Causes XOP encoding to be disabled for binary data types, such as Image
XmlList	Used to map a property to a list
XmlMimeType	Identifies a textual representation of the mime type for a property
XmlMixed	Identifies a multivalued property with mixed content
XmlNs	Identifies an XML namespace
XmlRegistry	Marks a class that has @XmlElementDecl
XmlRootElement	Maps a class or enumeration to an XML element
XmlSchema	Identifies a target namespace for a package
XmlSchemaType	Maps a Java type to a built-in schema type
XmlSchemaTypes	Acts as a container for multiple @XmlSchemaType annotations
XmlTransient	Flags a property that shouldn't be saved
XmlType	Maps a class or enumeration to a schema type
XmlValue	Allows the mapping of a class to a simple schema content or type

There are a lot of annotations listed in Table 6-2. There are also two other annotations, @XmlJavaTypeAdapter and @XmlJavaTypeAdapters, found in the javax.xml.bind.annotation. adapters package for custom marshalling. As JAXB 2.0 could be a book unto itself, I'm not going to describe how they all work together. What typically happens is that you write the XML Schema for your dataset, and the new xjc command-line tool generates the associated JavaBeans component classes. It places the annotations in the class files for you to get the right XML.

To demonstrate the xjc tool, Listing 6-2 shows a simple XML Schema document that describes courses as part of a student's schedule at a university. A schedule consists of a sequence of courses and a location. (This university restricts students to taking courses at a single campus location.) Each course has an ID, name, and description. The course location comes from an enumeration of north, south, east, and west.

Listing 6-2. *An XML Schema for a Course Schedule*

```
<schema xmlns="http://www.w3.org/2001/XMLSchema"
    xmlns:Revealed="http://www.jzventures.net"
    targetNamespace="http://www.jzventures.net"
>

    <element name="Schedule">
        <complexType>
            <sequence>
                <element name="course" type="Revealed:Course"
                    minOccurs="1" maxOccurs="unbounded"/>
                <element name="location" type="Revealed:Location"/>
            </sequence>
        </complexType>
    </element>

    <complexType name="Course">
        <sequence>
            <element name="courseId" type="string"/>
            <element name="name" type="string"/>
            <element name="description" type="string"/>
        </sequence>
    </complexType>

    <simpleType name="Location">
        <restriction base="string">
            <enumeration value="north"></enumeration>
            <enumeration value="south"></enumeration>
            <enumeration value="east"></enumeration>
            <enumeration value="west"></enumeration>
        </restriction>
    </simpleType>
</schema>
```

Tip Use a tool to generate the schema. It is best not to try to generate it by hand.

After you save the XML Schema, run it through the `xjc` tool to generate the associated Java classes.

```
> xjc course.xsd
parsing a schema...
compiling a schema...
net\jzventures\Course.java
net\jzventures\Location.java
net\jzventures\ObjectFactory.java
net\jzventures\Schedule.java
net\jzventures\package-info.java
```

As a result of running `xjc`, five class definitions were generated. Three of them are JavaBeans components. An object factory was also generated, along with a supporting class called `package-info`. The latter class is used to save off the namespace.

First look at the generated enumeration class, `Location`, shown in Listing 6-3.

Listing 6-3. *The Generated Enumeration Class*

```
//
// This file was generated by the JavaTM Architecture for XML Binding(JAXB) ➥
Reference Implementation, vJAXB 2.0 in JDK 1.6
// See <a href="http://java.sun.com/xml/jaxb">http://java.sun.com/xml/jaxb</a>
// Any modifications to this file will be lost upon recompilation of the source ➥
schema.
// Generated on: 2006.05.23 at 08:22:36 AM EDT
//


package net.jzventures;

import javax.xml.bind.annotation.XmlEnum;
import javax.xml.bind.annotation.XmlEnumValue;
```

```
/**
 * <p>Java class for Location.
 *
 * <p>The following schema fragment specifies the expected content contained ➡
within this class.
 * <p>
 * <pre>
 * &lt;simpleType name="Location">
 *   &lt;restriction base="{http://www.w3.org/2001/XMLSchema}string">
 *     &lt;enumeration value="north"/>
 *     &lt;enumeration value="south"/>
 *     &lt;enumeration value="east"/>
 *     &lt;enumeration value="west"/>
 *   &lt;/restriction>
 * &lt;/simpleType>
 * </pre>
 *
 */
@XmlEnum
public enum Location {

    @XmlEnumValue("east")
    EAST("east"),
    @XmlEnumValue("north")
    NORTH("north"),
    @XmlEnumValue("south")
    SOUTH("south"),
    @XmlEnumValue("west")
    WEST("west");
    private final String value;

    Location(String v) {
        value = v;
    }

    public String value() {
        return value;
    }
}
```

```
    public static Location fromValue(String v) {
        for (Location c: Location.values()) {
            if (c.value.equals(v)) {
                return c;
            }
        }
        throw new IllegalArgumentException(v.toString());
    }

}
```

Here, the namespace specified in the schema (targetNamespace) is used to identify the package name. The class name comes from the simpleType name of the schema, and gets an XmlEnum annotation. Each element of the enumeration then gets an XmlEnumValue.

Next up comes the complex type class Course, shown in Listing 6-4.

Listing 6-4. *The Generated Complex Type Class*

```
//
// This file was generated by the JavaTM Architecture for XML Binding(JAXB) ➥
Reference Implementation, vJAXB 2.0 in JDK 1.6
// See <a href="http://java.sun.com/xml/jaxb">http://java.sun.com/xml/jaxb</a>
// Any modifications to this file will be lost upon recompilation of the source ➥
schema.
// Generated on: 2006.05.23 at 08:38:43 AM EDT
//


package net.jzventures;

import javax.xml.bind.annotation.XmlAccessType;
import javax.xml.bind.annotation.XmlAccessorType;
import javax.xml.bind.annotation.XmlElement;
import javax.xml.bind.annotation.XmlType;


/**
 * <p>Java class for Course complex type.
 *
 * <p>The following schema fragment specifies the expected content contained ➥
within this class.
 *
```

```
 * <pre>
 * &lt;complexType name="Course">
 *   &lt;complexContent>
 *     &lt;restriction base="{http://www.w3.org/2001/XMLSchema}anyType">
 *       &lt;sequence>
 *         &lt;element name="courseId" ➥
type="{http://www.w3.org/2001/XMLSchema}string"/>
 *         &lt;element name="name" type="{http://www.w3.org/2001/XMLSchema}string"/>
 *         &lt;element name="description" ➥
type="{http://www.w3.org/2001/XMLSchema}string"/>
 *       &lt;/sequence>
 *     &lt;/restriction>
 *   &lt;/complexContent>
 * &lt;/complexType>
 * </pre>
 *
 *
 */
@XmlAccessorType(XmlAccessType.FIELD)
@XmlType(name = "Course", propOrder = {
    "courseId",
    "name",
    "description"
})
public class Course {

    @XmlElement(required = true)
    protected String courseId;
    @XmlElement(required = true)
    protected String name;
    @XmlElement(required = true)
    protected String description;

    /**
     * Gets the value of the courseId property.
     *
     * @return
     *     possible object is
     *     {@link String }
     *
     */
```

```java
public String getCourseId() {
    return courseId;
}

/**
 * Sets the value of the courseId property.
 *
 * @param value
 *     allowed object is
 *     {@link String }
 *
 */
public void setCourseId(String value) {
    this.courseId = value;
}

/**
 * Gets the value of the name property.
 *
 * @return
 *     possible object is
 *     {@link String }
 *
 */
public String getName() {
    return name;
}

/**
 * Sets the value of the name property.
 *
 * @param value
 *     allowed object is
 *     {@link String }
 *
 */
public void setName(String value) {
    this.name = value;
}
```

```
    /**
     * Gets the value of the description property.
     *
     * @return
     *     possible object is
     *     {@link String }
     *
     */
    public String getDescription() {
        return description;
    }


    /**
     * Sets the value of the description property.
     *
     * @param value
     *     allowed object is
     *     {@link String }
     *
     */
    public void setDescription(String value) {
        this.description = value;
    }


}
```

The order of elements within the schema defined the order of properties for the JavaBeans component. The getter and setter methods were generated for all three properties here, along with javadocs. Again, the class name came from the initial complex type name.

The Schedule class in Listing 6-5 represents the third JavaBeans component generated.

Listing 6-5. *The Generated Top-Level-Element Class*

```
//
// This file was generated by the JavaTM Architecture for XML Binding(JAXB) ➥
Reference Implementation, vJAXB 2.0 in JDK 1.6
// See <a href="http://java.sun.com/xml/jaxb">http://java.sun.com/xml/jaxb</a>
// Any modifications to this file will be lost upon recompilation of the source ➥
schema.
// Generated on: 2006.05.23 at 09:11:23 AM EDT
//
```

```
package net.jzventures;

import java.util.ArrayList;
import java.util.List;
import javax.xml.bind.annotation.XmlAccessType;
import javax.xml.bind.annotation.XmlAccessorType;
import javax.xml.bind.annotation.XmlElement;
import javax.xml.bind.annotation.XmlRootElement;
import javax.xml.bind.annotation.XmlType;


/**
 * <p>Java class for Schedule element declaration.
 *
 * <p>The following schema fragment specifies the expected content contained ➡
within this class.
 *
 * <pre>
 * &lt;element name="Schedule">
 *   &lt;complexType>
 *     &lt;complexContent>
 *       &lt;restriction base="{http://www.w3.org/2001/XMLSchema}anyType">
 *         &lt;sequence>
 *           &lt;element name="course" type="{http://www.jzventures.net}Course" ➡
maxOccurs="unbounded"/>
 *           &lt;element name="location" ➡
type="{http://www.jzventures.net}Location"/>
 *         &lt;/sequence>
 *       &lt;/restriction>
 *     &lt;/complexContent>
 *   &lt;/complexType>
 * &lt;/element>
 * </pre>
 *
 *
 */
@XmlAccessorType(XmlAccessType.FIELD)
@XmlType(name = "", propOrder = {
    "course",
```

```java
        "location"
})
@XmlRootElement(name = "Schedule")
public class Schedule {

    @XmlElement(required = true)
    protected List<Course> course;
    @XmlElement(required = true)
    protected Location location;

    /**
     * Gets the value of the course property.
     *
     * <p>
     * This accessor method returns a reference to the live list,
     * not a snapshot. Therefore any modification you make to the
     * returned list will be present inside the JAXB object.
     * This is why there is not a <CODE>set</CODE> method for the course property.
     *
     * <p>
     * For example, to add a new item, do as follows:
     * <pre>
     *    getCourse().add(newItem);
     * </pre>
     *
     *
     * <p>
     * Objects of the following type(s) are allowed in the list
     * {@link Course }
     *
     *
     */
    public List<Course> getCourse() {
        if (course == null) {
            course = new ArrayList<Course>();
        }
        return this.course;
    }
```

```
/**
 * Gets the value of the location property.
 *
 * @return
 *     possible object is
 *     {@link Location }
 *
 */
public Location getLocation() {
    return location;
}

/**
 * Sets the value of the location property.
 *
 * @param value
 *     allowed object is
 *     {@link Location }
 *
 */
public void setLocation(Location value) {
    this.location = value;
}

}
```

Again, accessor methods are generated for the component properties, with the class name coming from the element name. Since the course property is a List object, no setter method is provided. You must get the list and add/remove elements from it yourself to adjust the collection.

The final class, ObjectFactory in Listing 6-6, just offers factory methods to create Course and Schedule objects. The Course and Schedule objects are those elements that can be contained within the outermost object; but there is no factory method for the outermost object itself.

Listing 6-6. *The Generated ObjectFactory Class*

```
//
// This file was generated by the JavaTM Architecture for XML Binding(JAXB) ➥
Reference Implementation, vJAXB 2.0 in JDK 1.6
// See <a href="http://java.sun.com/xml/jaxb">http://java.sun.com/xml/jaxb</a>
```

```
// Any modifications to this file will be lost upon recompilation of the source ➥
schema.
// Generated on: 2006.05.23 at 08:38:43 AM EDT
//


package net.jzventures;

import javax.xml.bind.annotation.XmlRegistry;


/**
 * This object contains factory methods for each
 * Java content interface and Java element interface
 * generated in the net.jzventures package.
 * <p>An ObjectFactory allows you to programatically
 * construct new instances of the Java representation
 * for XML content. The Java representation of XML
 * content can consist of schema derived interfaces
 * and classes representing the binding of schema
 * type definitions, element declarations and model
 * groups.  Factory methods for each of these are
 * provided in this class.
 *
 */
@XmlRegistry
public class ObjectFactory {


    /**
     * Create a new ObjectFactory that can be used to create new instances of ➥
schema derived classes for package: net.jzventures
     *
     */
    public ObjectFactory() {
    }

    /**
     * Create an instance of {@link Course }
     *
     */
```

```
    public Course createCourse() {
        return new Course();
    }


    /**
     * Create an instance of {@link Schedule }
     *
     */
    public Schedule createSchedule() {
        return new Schedule();
    }


}
```

■**Note** There is no factory method provided for Location because it is an enumeration.

At this point, you could use the Course, Location, and Schedule classes to create a schedule loaded with courses for a student, and then dump it to XML; or you could create the XML file and read it in, in order to get the Schedule with its associated Course and Location objects, as defined in the XML. Reading content in (unmarshalling) is similar to the earlier marshalling example shown in Listing 6-1, but instead requires you to get the Unmarshaller from the JAXBContext, instead of the Marshaller.

```
    JAXBContext jc = JAXBContext.newInstance();
    Unmarshaller u = jc.createUnmarshaller();
    Schedule s = (Schedule)u.unmarshal(new File("schedule.xml"));
```

For more information on JAXB, see its project page at https://jaxb.dev.java.net. Several tutorials that offer more explanations on the technology are offered there. For those coming to Java SE 6 from a Java EE environment, the API here should already be familiar, as much of this has been around since 2004.

The javax.xml.crypto Package

JSR 105 created the javax.xml.crypto package as part of the XML Digital Signature APIs specification. The XML digital signature specification is defined by the W3C (and available from www.w3.org/2000/09/xmldsig). This is just a Java implementation of the specification. The JSR and its associated API has been final since June of 2005.

While the `javax.xml.crypto` package offers several packages and isn't that small, there are really just two key tasks here that you need to know how to do: how to sign an XML document, and how to validate that signature. To examine this, you'll create a fictitious SOAP message to be signed and validated. Many of the APIs necessary for the task are standard Java security APIs, not specific to the newer XML digital signature APIs.

The basic process of signing is shown in Listing 6-7. You need something to sign, so get a DOM node from a SOAP message, or from some other place. Next, generate the XML signature with the help of a DSA key pair. The last two method calls are the real work to sign and validate. Obviously, in real life you wouldn't do everything at one time—however, I believe the tasks are separated out enough so that you can understand things fully and will be able to reuse the pieces in your own programs.

Listing 6-7. *Framework for Signing an XML Document*

```
SOAPMessage soapMessage = createSOAPMessage();

SOAPPart soapPart = soapMessage.getSOAPPart();
Source source = soapPart.getContent();
Node root = generateDOM(source);

KeyPair keypair = generateDSAKeyPair();
XMLSignature sig = generateXMLSignature(keypair);

signTree(root, keypair.getPrivate(), sig);

boolean valid = validateXMLSignature(keypair.getPublic(), root, sig);
```

The first task of generating the SOAP message is shown in Listing 6-8. It uses the new `javax.xml.soap` package to generate the message (more on this package in Chapter 7). There's nothing really special here—just a bogus message with a body area identified by a `Body` attribute to be used later.

Listing 6-8. *Generating the SOAP Message*

```
  private static SOAPMessage createSOAPMessage() throws SOAPException {
    SOAPMessage soapMessage = MessageFactory.newInstance().createMessage();
    SOAPPart soapPart = soapMessage.getSOAPPart();
    SOAPEnvelope soapEnvelope = soapPart.getEnvelope();
```

```
SOAPHeader soapHeader = soapEnvelope.getHeader();
SOAPHeaderElement headerElement = soapHeader.addHeaderElement(
  soapEnvelope.createName("Signature", "SOAP-SEC",
  "http://schemas.xmlsoap.org/soap/security/2000-12"));

SOAPBody soapBody = soapEnvelope.getBody();
soapBody.addAttribute(soapEnvelope.createName("id", "SOAP-SEC",
  "http://schemas.xmlsoap.org/soap/security/2000-12"), "Body");
Name bodyName =soapEnvelope.createName("FooBar", "z", "http://example.com");
SOAPBodyElement gltp = soapBody.addBodyElement(bodyName);

return soapMessage;
}
```

Listing 6-9 converts the SOAP message content to a DOM (Document Object Model). This does not just take the results of createSOAPMessage(), but instead works with the content from SOAPPart. None of these concepts are new to Java 6, so I'll spare you the details.

Listing 6-9. *Generating the DOM*

```
private static Node generateDOM(Source source)
    throws ParserConfigurationException, SAXException, IOException {

  Node root;
  if (source instanceof DOMSource) {
    root = ((DOMSource)source).getNode();
  } else if (source instanceof SAXSource) {
    InputSource inSource = ((SAXSource)source).getInputSource();
    DocumentBuilderFactory dbf = DocumentBuilderFactory.newInstance();
    dbf.setNamespaceAware(true);  // so parser supports namespaces
    DocumentBuilder db = null;

    synchronized (dbf) {
      db = dbf.newDocumentBuilder();
    }

    Document doc = db.parse(inSource);
    root = (Node) doc.getDocumentElement();
```

```
  } else {
    throw new IllegalArgumentException(
      "Class type: " + source.getClass().getName());
  }

  return root;
}
```

The last of the "old" code usage is Listing 6-10, in which a Digital Signature Algorithm (DSA) key pair is generated to do the XML tree signing. From this key pair, you would typically share the public key so that others can validate items that you've signed. It is this PublicKey that is passed into the final validateXMLSignature() method.

Listing 6-10. *Generating the DSA Key Pair*

```
private static KeyPair generateDSAKeyPair() throws NoSuchAlgorithmException {
  KeyPairGenerator kpg = KeyPairGenerator.getInstance("DSA");
  kpg.initialize(1024, new SecureRandom());
  return kpg.generateKeyPair();
}
```

At this point, the code starts to get a little more interesting. You need an XMLSignature to sign the tree. This class is found in the new javax.xml.crypto.dsig package, and you get it with the help of an XMLSignatureFactory. Its getInstance() method has several varieties. By default, it fetches the default DOM mechanism with no arguments. You can also ask for the DOM explicitly, as shown in Listing 6-11. Two other versions let you explicitly specify the provider. Once you have the factory, you need to configure it before asking to create the new XMLSignature with newXMLSignature(). The W3C Recommendation for XML-Signature Syntax and Processing documentation (www.w3.org/TR/xmldsig-core) offers information on available configuration options, though you'll need to look for the specific Java configuration classes to match.

Listing 6-11. *Generating the XML Signature*

```
private static XMLSignature generateXMLSignature(KeyPair keypair)
    throws NoSuchAlgorithmException, InvalidAlgorithmParameterException,
      KeyException {
  XMLSignatureFactory sigFactory = XMLSignatureFactory.getInstance("DOM");
  Reference ref = sigFactory.newReference("#Body",
    sigFactory.newDigestMethod(DigestMethod.SHA1, null));
  SignedInfo signedInfo = sigFactory.newSignedInfo(
    sigFactory.newCanonicalizationMethod(
```

```
            CanonicalizationMethod.INCLUSIVE_WITH_COMMENTS,
            (C14NMethodParameterSpec) null),
            sigFactory.newSignatureMethod(SignatureMethod.DSA_SHA1, null),
            Collections.singletonList(ref));
        KeyInfoFactory kif = sigFactory.getKeyInfoFactory();
        KeyValue kv = kif.newKeyValue(keypair.getPublic());
        KeyInfo keyInfo = kif.newKeyInfo(Collections.singletonList(kv));

        return sigFactory.newXMLSignature(signedInfo, keyInfo);
    }
```

By now, the hard part is over. Listing 6-12 shows how to identify where to insert the signature and connect back to the previously used body ID. The last sig.sign() call is what does the signing.

Listing 6-12. *The Signing Tree*

```
    private static void signTree(Node root, PrivateKey privateKey, XMLSignature sig)
        throws MarshalException, XMLSignatureException {

        Element envelope = getFirstChildElement(root);
        Element header = getFirstChildElement(envelope);
        DOMSignContext sigContext = new DOMSignContext(privateKey, header);
        sigContext.putNamespacePrefix(XMLSignature.XMLNS, "ds");
        sigContext.setIdAttributeNS(getNextSiblingElement(header),
            "http://schemas.xmlsoap.org/soap/security/2000-12","id");
        sig.sign(sigContext);
    }
```

Similar to signing, validation (see Listing 6-13) isn't that complicated once you have the necessary pieces. Again, this requires you to find the signature element before locating the body element to validate. Finally, the validate() method of XMLSignature is called to see if the tree passes.

Listing 6-13. *Validating the XML Signature*

```
    private static boolean validateXMLSignature(
        PublicKey publicKey, Node root, XMLSignature sig)
            throws XMLSignatureException {
```

```
      Element envelope = getFirstChildElement(root);
      Element header = getFirstChildElement(envelope);
      Element sigElement = getFirstChildElement(header);
      DOMValidateContext valContext = new DOMValidateContext(publicKey, sigElement);
      valContext.setIdAttributeNS(getNextSiblingElement(header),
        "http://schemas.xmlsoap.org/soap/security/2000-12", "id");
      return sig.validate(valContext);
    }
```

Listing 6-14 shows the complete program in action. A couple of DOM tree dumps are shown before and after the tree is signed.

Listing 6-14. *The Complete XML Signing Example*

```
import java.io.*;
import java.security.*;
import java.util.*;

import javax.xml.crypto.*;
import javax.xml.crypto.dsig.*;
import javax.xml.crypto.dom.*;
import javax.xml.crypto.dsig.dom.*;
import javax.xml.crypto.dsig.keyinfo.*;
import javax.xml.crypto.dsig.spec.*;
import javax.xml.soap.*;
import javax.xml.parsers.*;
import javax.xml.transform.*;
import javax.xml.transform.dom.*;
import javax.xml.transform.sax.*;
import javax.xml.transform.stream.*;

import org.w3c.dom.*;
import org.w3c.dom.Node;
import org.xml.sax.*;

public class Signing {

  public static void main(String[] args) throws Exception {

    SOAPMessage soapMessage = createSOAPMessage();
```

```java
    SOAPPart soapPart = soapMessage.getSOAPPart();
    Source source = soapPart.getContent();
    Node root = generateDOM(source);

    dumpDocument(root);

    KeyPair keypair = generateDSAKeyPair();
    XMLSignature sig = generateXMLSignature(keypair);

    System.out.println("Signing the message...");
    signTree(root, keypair.getPrivate(), sig);

    dumpDocument(root);

    System.out.println("Validate the signature...");
    boolean valid = validateXMLSignature(keypair.getPublic(), root, sig);
    System.out.println("Signature valid? " + valid);
}

private static SOAPMessage createSOAPMessage() throws SOAPException {
    SOAPMessage soapMessage = MessageFactory.newInstance().createMessage();
    SOAPPart soapPart = soapMessage.getSOAPPart();
    SOAPEnvelope soapEnvelope = soapPart.getEnvelope();

    SOAPHeader soapHeader = soapEnvelope.getHeader();
    SOAPHeaderElement headerElement = soapHeader.addHeaderElement(
        soapEnvelope.createName("Signature", "SOAP-SEC",
        "http://schemas.xmlsoap.org/soap/security/2000-12"));

    SOAPBody soapBody = soapEnvelope.getBody();
    soapBody.addAttribute(soapEnvelope.createName("id", "SOAP-SEC",
        "http://schemas.xmlsoap.org/soap/security/2000-12"), "Body");
    Name bodyName =soapEnvelope.createName("FooBar", "z", "http://example.com");
    SOAPBodyElement gltp = soapBody.addBodyElement(bodyName);

    return soapMessage;
}

private static Node generateDOM(Source source)
    throws ParserConfigurationException, SAXException, IOException {
```

```java
  Node root;
  if (source instanceof DOMSource) {
    root = ((DOMSource)source).getNode();
  } else if (source instanceof SAXSource) {
    InputSource inSource = ((SAXSource)source).getInputSource();
    DocumentBuilderFactory dbf = DocumentBuilderFactory.newInstance();
    dbf.setNamespaceAware(true);
    DocumentBuilder db = null;

    synchronized (dbf) {
      db = dbf.newDocumentBuilder();
    }

    Document doc = db.parse(inSource);
    root = (Node) doc.getDocumentElement();

  } else {
    throw new IllegalArgumentException(
      "Class type: " + source.getClass().getName());
  }

  return root;
}

private static KeyPair generateDSAKeyPair() throws NoSuchAlgorithmException {
  KeyPairGenerator kpg = KeyPairGenerator.getInstance("DSA");
  kpg.initialize(1024, new SecureRandom());
  return kpg.generateKeyPair();
}

private static XMLSignature generateXMLSignature(KeyPair keypair)
    throws NoSuchAlgorithmException, InvalidAlgorithmParameterException,
      KeyException {
  XMLSignatureFactory sigFactory = XMLSignatureFactory.getInstance();
  Reference ref = sigFactory.newReference("#Body",
    sigFactory.newDigestMethod(DigestMethod.SHA1, null));
  SignedInfo signedInfo = sigFactory.newSignedInfo(
    sigFactory.newCanonicalizationMethod(
    CanonicalizationMethod.INCLUSIVE_WITH_COMMENTS,
    (C14NMethodParameterSpec) null),
    sigFactory.newSignatureMethod(SignatureMethod.DSA_SHA1, null),
    Collections.singletonList(ref));
```

```
    KeyInfoFactory kif = sigFactory.getKeyInfoFactory();
    KeyValue kv = kif.newKeyValue(keypair.getPublic());
    KeyInfo keyInfo = kif.newKeyInfo(Collections.singletonList(kv));

    return sigFactory.newXMLSignature(signedInfo, keyInfo);
}

private static void signTree(Node root, PrivateKey privateKey, XMLSignature sig)
    throws MarshalException, XMLSignatureException {

  Element envelope = getFirstChildElement(root);
  Element header = getFirstChildElement(envelope);
  DOMSignContext sigContext = new DOMSignContext(privateKey, header);
  sigContext.putNamespacePrefix(XMLSignature.XMLNS, "ds");
  sigContext.setIdAttributeNS(getNextSiblingElement(header),
    "http://schemas.xmlsoap.org/soap/security/2000-12","id");
  sig.sign(sigContext);
}

private static boolean validateXMLSignature(
    PublicKey publicKey, Node root, XMLSignature sig)
      throws XMLSignatureException {

  Element envelope = getFirstChildElement(root);
  Element header = getFirstChildElement(envelope);
  Element sigElement = getFirstChildElement(header);
  DOMValidateContext valContext = new DOMValidateContext(publicKey, sigElement);
  valContext.setIdAttributeNS(getNextSiblingElement(header),
    "http://schemas.xmlsoap.org/soap/security/2000-12", "id");
  return sig.validate(valContext);
}

private static void dumpDocument(Node root) throws TransformerException {

  Console console = System.console();
  console.printf("%n");
  Transformer transformer = TransformerFactory.newInstance().newTransformer();
  transformer.setOutputProperty(OutputKeys.INDENT, "yes");
  transformer.transform(new DOMSource(root), new StreamResult(console.writer()));
  console.printf("%n");
}
```

```
    private static Element getFirstChildElement(Node node) {

      Node child = node.getFirstChild();
      while ((child != null) && (child.getNodeType() != Node.ELEMENT_NODE)) {
        child = child.getNextSibling();
      }
      return (Element) child;
    }

    public static Element getNextSiblingElement(Node node) {

      Node sibling = node.getNextSibling();
      while ((sibling != null) && (sibling.getNodeType() != Node.ELEMENT_NODE)) {
        sibling = sibling.getNextSibling();
      }
      return (Element) sibling;
    }
}
```

When run, you'll see both tree dumps, and hopefully a note showing that the validation passed. The "before" tree, shown following, is rather small:

```
<?xml version="1.0" encoding="UTF-8" standalone="no"?>
<SOAP-ENV:Envelope xmlns:SOAP-ENV="http://schemas.xmlsoap.org/soap/envelope/">
<SOAP-ENV:Header>
<SOAP-SEC:Signature xmlns:SOAP-SEC=➡
"http://schemas.xmlsoap.org/soap/security/2000-12"/>
</SOAP-ENV:Header>
<SOAP-ENV:Body xmlns:SOAP-SEC=➡
"http://schemas.xmlsoap.org/soap/security/2000-12" SOAP-SEC:id="Body">
<z:FooBar xmlns:z="http://example.com"/>
</SOAP-ENV:Body>
</SOAP-ENV:Envelope>
```

The "after" tree has grown somewhat. Your output is apt to be different, unless
SecureRandom generated the same random number. All the digital signature–related fields
have a namespace of ds because of the earlier putNamespacePrefix() call.

```
<?xml version="1.0" encoding="UTF-8" standalone="no"?>
<SOAP-ENV:Envelope xmlns:SOAP-ENV="http://schemas.xmlsoap.org/soap/envelope/">
<SOAP-ENV:Header>
<SOAP-SEC:Signature xmlns:SOAP-SEC=➡
"http://schemas.xmlsoap.org/soap/security/200-12"/>
```

```
<ds:Signature xmlns:ds="http://www.w3.org/2000/09/xmldsig#">
<ds:SignedInfo>
<ds:CanonicalizationMethod Algorithm=➥
"http://www.w3.org/TR/2001/REC-xml-c14n-2010315#WithComments"/>
<ds:SignatureMethod Algorithm="http://www.w3.org/2000/09/xmldsig#dsa-sha1"/>
<ds:Reference URI="#Body">
<ds:DigestMethod Algorithm="http://www.w3.org/2000/09/xmldsig#sha1"/>
<ds:DigestValue>9xOmZhajy9dHKuIXh7bmOkhuC7M=</ds:DigestValue>
</ds:Reference>
</ds:SignedInfo>
<ds:SignatureValue>KF36gdqKiFN6J4Yzj8tI9jtuenlQbtT95hdbS5olBJcPByp2BjAupA==</ds
SignatureValue>
<ds:KeyInfo>
<ds:KeyValue>
<ds:DSAKeyValue>
<ds:P>/X9TgR11EilS3OqcLuzk5/YRt1I870QAwx4/gLZRJmlFXUAiUftZPY1Y+r/F9bow9subVWzXguA
HTRv8mZgt2uZUKWkn5/oBHsQIsJPu6nX/rfGG/g7V+fGqKYVDwT7g/bTxR7DAjVUE1oWkTL2dfOu
K2HXKu/yIgMZndFIAcc=</ds:P>
<ds:Q>l2BQjxUjC8yykrmCouuEC/BYHPU=</ds:Q>
<ds:G>9+GghdabPd7LvKtcNrhXuXmUr7v6OuqC+VdMCzOHgmdRWVeOutRZT+ZxBxCBgLRJFnEj6EwoFO3
zwkyjMim4TwWeotUfIOo4KOuHiuzpnWRbqN/C/ohNWLx+2J6ASQ7zKTxvqhRkImog9/hWuWfBpKL
Zl6Ae1UlZAFMO/7PSSo=</ds:G>
<ds:Y>pX4PwF5u7xqoIv4wgk/zq7CaNHwLgFXxZncbqHU9vL1oZttOmADKKSsRsnLsHw67Q7KktzN16am
o/2YHCGJ4r4iTNTxiOgAlGRg6CD/Em4c5tRcu/Qi8/Ck31BIT2B8EgzcY1SfXc1gqLRYFNwfLUBp
mOXJ/8JJ4n/mCZp+PIw=</ds:Y>
</ds:DSAKeyValue>
</ds:KeyValue>
</ds:KeyInfo>
</ds:Signature>
</SOAP-ENV:Header>
<SOAP-ENV:Body xmlns:SOAP-SEC=➥
"http://schemas.xmlsoap.org/soap/security/2000-12 SOAP-SEC:id="Body">
<z:FooBar xmlns:z="http://example.com"/>
</SOAP-ENV:Body>
</SOAP-ENV:Envelope>
```

That's pretty much it for the basics of the XML Digital Signature API and JSR 105. For more information on the API, see the Java Web Services Developer Pack tutorial, available at http://java.sun.com/webservices/docs/1.6/tutorial/doc/XMLDigitalSignatureAPI8.html. Just realize that since you're using Java 6, you don't need to install any supplemental packages that might be mentioned.

The javax.xml.stream Package

Another facet of the new XML-related APIs in Java 6 has to do with JSR 173 and the Streaming API for XML, or StAX. It is like SAX parsing, but works on pulling events from the parser, instead of the parser throwing events at you. It definitely does not follow the tree model of DOM, but does allow you to pause the parsing and skip ahead if necessary; and unlike SAX, it does allow writing of XML documents, not just reading.

There are two parts to the StAX API: a Cursor API for walking the document from beginning to end, and an Iterator API for handling events in the order that they appear in the source document. You'll see how to use both, but first you need an XML document to read. Listing 6-15 shows one that represents a series of points, with x and y coordinates for each.

Listing 6-15. *A Simple XML Document*

```
<?xml version="1.0" encoding="UTF-8" standalone="yes"?>
<points>
    <point>
        <x>1</x>
        <y>2</y>
    </point>
    <point>
        <x>3</x>
        <y>4</y>
    </point>
    <point>
        <x>5</x>
        <y>6</y>
    </point>
</points>
```

Listing 6-16 shows a demonstration of the Cursor API. There is no Cursor class for the Streaming API for XML—it is just called that for its manner of going through the XML file. The class basically gets an XMLStreamReader from the XMLInputFactory and then starts looping through the stream. For each event the system runs across, the cursor stops for processing. You can check the event type against one of the XMLEvent interface constants, or rely on methods like isStartElement() or isCharacters() of the same interface to test for event type. By working with the integer constants, you can create a switch statement like the one in Listing 6-16 for handling different element types.

Listing 6-16. *Cursor API Usage*

```java
import java.io.*;
import javax.xml.stream.*;
import javax.xml.stream.events.*;

public class CursorRead {
  public static void main(String args[]) throws Exception {
    Console console = System.console();
    XMLInputFactory xmlif = XMLInputFactory.newInstance();
    XMLStreamReader xmlsr = xmlif.createXMLStreamReader(
      new FileReader("points.xml"));
    int eventType;
    while (xmlsr.hasNext()) {
      eventType = xmlsr.next();
      switch (eventType) {
        case XMLEvent.START_ELEMENT:
          console.printf("%s", xmlsr.getName());
          break;
        case XMLEvent.CHARACTERS:
          console.printf("\t>%s", xmlsr.getText());
          break;
        default:
          break;
      }
    }
  }
}
```

The Cursor API and its XMLStreamReader interface don't implement the Iterator interface; however, the events are iterated through in the same way—with hasNext() and next() methods. Be sure to call next() after hasNext() has returned true to move to the next element in the stream.

Running Listing 6-16 against the XML file in Listing 6-15 produces the following results:

```
> java CursorRead
points
   point
      x       1
      y       2
```

```
point
    x        3
    y        4


point
    x        5
    y        6
```

This is nothing fancy, but it does walk through the tree for you. Feel free to add more output options for different event types.

The second half of the StAX API is the Iterator API (Listing 6-17), which works slightly differently from the Cursor API. Instead of having to go back to the stream to get the associated data for each element you get from the cursor, you instead get an XMLEvent back as you walk through the iteration. Each XMLEvent thus has its associated data with it, like the name for the start element or the text data for the characters.

Listing 6-17. *Iterator API Usage*

```java
import java.io.*;
import javax.xml.stream.*;
import javax.xml.stream.events.*;

public class IteratorRead {
  public static void main(String args[]) throws Exception {
    Console console = System.console();
    XMLInputFactory xmlif = XMLInputFactory.newInstance();
    XMLEventReader xmler = xmlif.createXMLEventReader(
      new FileReader("points.xml"));
    XMLEvent event;
    while (xmler.hasNext()) {
      event = xmler.nextEvent();
      if (event.isStartElement()) {
        console.printf("%s", event.asStartElement().getName());
      } else if (event.isCharacters()) {
        console.printf("\t%s", event.asCharacters().getData());
      }
    }
  }
}
```

The output produced with Listing 6-17 is identical to that of 6-16. While the output is the same, there are many differences between the two APIs. First, the Iterator API allows you to peek ahead without actually reading the stream. This allows you to check ahead to see what to do next before committing to reading the element. While the Cursor API is more efficient in memory-constrained environments, the Iterator API supports modifications, and is best when pipelining streams. If the Iterator API is sufficient, it is typically best to stick with that for desktop and web applications.

For more information on StAX parsing, visit its java.net home at `https://sjsxp.dev.java.net`. The Java Web Services tutorial (`http://java.sun.com/webservices/docs/1.6/tutorial/doc`) includes a good introduction to the technology, too.

Summary

If you've been doing Java EE–related development, many of the new XML-related APIs for Mustang won't be new and different for you. All they are now is standard with Java SE. The JAXB 2.0 libraries give you Java-to-XML and XML-to-Java data bindings, the XML Digital Signature API gives you signing of your XML files, and the StAX processing gives you yet another way to parse your XML files—this time in a streaming fashion with the possibility to write and not just read the stream.

The next chapter takes you to even more familiar APIs for the Java EE developer: those related to web services. With the ever-growing popularity of web services, they aren't just for enterprise developers anymore. Thanks to their inclusion in Java 6, you too can use them without adding any optional packages to your Java SE environment.

CHAPTER 7

■■■

Web Services

Who doesn't use web services these days? Due to the increasing popularity of web services, the Java APIs for taking advantage of the functionality are moving from the latest Java EE release into the Java SE 6 platform. In other words, there are no add-on kits for web services, and both platforms have the same API. Mustang adds a handful of different web services–related APIs to the standard tool chest: Web Services Metadata for the Java Platform with JSR 181, the Java API for XML-Based Web Services (JAX-WS) 2.0 via JSR 224, and the SOAP with Attachments API for Java (SAAJ) 1.3 as part of JSR 67.

Before continuing with the chapter, it is necessary to point out one very important point: this is not a book about web services. I've seen 1,000-plus-page books on web services that still require you to understand some level of XML, SOAP, or some other Java API to take full advantage of the described capabilities. In this chapter, I'll do my best to show examples of using the new APIs in the context of a Java SE program. If you need more information about creating web services, consider getting one of Apress's other titles or some of the many online tutorials on the topic. You will need to "convert" the online tutorial to Mustang, but the web services APIs are pretty much the same, just in a new environment: Java SE, instead of Java EE.

The packages associated with the three web services APIs are new to Java SE, so no need for tables showing the differences between Java 5 and 6. The JAX-WS API is found in the `javax.xml.ws` packages, the SAAJ classes are in `javax.xml.soap`, and the Web Services Metadata classes are found under `javax.jws`.

The javax.jws Package

JSR 181 and its specification of Web Services Metadata for the Java Platform provide a mechanism to utilize annotations in classes to design and develop web services. For those unfamiliar with annotations, they were introduced with J2SE 5.0 and have been expanded somewhat with Java 6. They are described more fully in Chapter 10; but they essentially allow you to add @tags to classes, methods, and properties to describe associated metadata. A parser can then locate the tags and act appropriately; though when that action happens is dependent upon the tag itself.

The two packages involved here are javax.jws and javax.jws.soap. Both packages only define enumerations and annotations. There are neither classes nor interfaces here. By importing the appropriate package for the annotations, you can annotate the classes that represent web services, and their methods, as shown in Listing 7-1. Be sure to include a package statement. If you don't, when you run the wsgen tool later, you'll get an error message, as follows:

```
modeler error: @javax.jws.Webservice annotated classes that do not belong to a
    package must have the @javax.jws.Webservice.targetNamespace element.
    Class: HelloService
```

Listing 7-1. *An Annotated Hello World Service*

```
package net.zukowski.revealed;

import javax.jws.WebService;
import javax.jws.WebMethod;

@WebService
public class HelloService {

  @WebMethod
  public String helloWorld() {
    return "Hello, World";
  }
}
```

There are two basic annotations specified here: @WebService and @WebMethod. The @WebService annotation identifies the HelloService class as a web service. If not specified otherwise, the @WebService annotation assumes the name is that of the class. You can also specify a namespace, service name, WSDL location, and endpoint interface.

But what can you do with the source file? Running the javac compiler against the source just spits out a .class file—nothing else special. You still need to do that. But after compiling the class, you also need to run the wsgen command-line tool (wsgen is short for web service generator).

The wsgen tool generates a handful of source files and then compiles. Since the package name of the example here is net.zukowski.revealed, the new classes are generated into the net/zukowski/revealed/jaxws directory. Listings 7-2 and 7-3 show the source for the classes generated from running the following command:

```
> wsgen -cp . net.zukowski.revealed.HelloService
```

Listing 7-2. *The First Generated Class for the Web Service*

```java
package net.zukowski.revealed.jaxws;

import javax.xml.bind.annotation.XmlAccessType;
import javax.xml.bind.annotation.XmlAccessorType;
import javax.xml.bind.annotation.XmlRootElement;
import javax.xml.bind.annotation.XmlType;

@XmlRootElement(name = "helloWorld", namespace = "http://revealed.zukowski.net/")
@XmlAccessorType(XmlAccessType.FIELD)
@XmlType(name = "helloWorld", namespace = "http://revealed.zukowski.net/")
public class HelloWorld {
}
```

Listing 7-3. *The Second Generated Class for the Web Service*

```java
package net.zukowski.revealed.jaxws;

import javax.xml.bind.annotation.XmlAccessType;
import javax.xml.bind.annotation.XmlAccessorType;
import javax.xml.bind.annotation.XmlElement;
import javax.xml.bind.annotation.XmlRootElement;
import javax.xml.bind.annotation.XmlType;

@XmlRootElement(name = "helloWorldResponse", ➥
    namespace = "http://revealed.zukowski.net/")
@XmlAccessorType(XmlAccessType.FIELD)
@XmlType(name = "helloWorldResponse", namespace = "http://revealed.zukowski.net/")
public class HelloWorldResponse {

    @XmlElement(name = "return", namespace = "")
    private String _return;

    /**
     *
     * @return
     *     returns String
     */
    public String get_return() {
        return this._return;
    }
```

```
    /**
     *
     * @param _return
     *     the value for the _return property
     */
    public void set_return(String _return) {
        this._return = _return;
    }
}
```

There is certainly much more you can do with annotations here. In fact, the annotations found in the javax.jws.soap package are where you get the SOAP bindings, which takes us to the next section.

The javax.xml.ws and javax.xml.soap Packages

The JAX-WS API is very closely associated with JAXB. Where JAXB is the Java-to-XML mapping, and vice versa, JAX-WS is the mapping of Java objects to and from the Web Services Description Language (WSDL). Together, with the help of the SAAJ, the trio gives you the API stack for web services.

What does all that mean? With the help of last chapter's JAXB, you can use the SAAJ and JAX-WS APIs to generate SOAP messages to connect to web services to get results. You're not going to deploy web services with Mustang. Instead, you're going to connect to preexisting services to get answers. The available APIs are what you get with Java EE 5.

SOAP Messages

In the last chapter, you saw an example creating a SOAP message. The javax.xml.soap package provides a MessageFactory, from which you get an instance to create the message.

```
SOAPMessage soapMessage = MessageFactory.newInstance().createMessage();
```

This generates a SOAP 1.2 message format. If you need to create a message for the SOAP 1.1 protocol, you can pass the protocol name to the createMessage() method.

```
SOAPMessage soapMessage =
  MessageFactory.newInstance().createMessage(SOAPConstants.SOAP_1_1_PROTOCOL);
```

The SOAP message in turn consists of a series of other objects: SOAPPart, SOAPEnvelope, SOAPBody, and SOAPHeader. All of these bits are in XML format. To include non-XML data within the message, you would use one or more AttachmentPart type objects. These are created from either an Activation Framework DataHandler, or directly from an `Object` and mime type. Think of e-mail attachments here. There is built-in support in SAAJ 1.3 for mime types of type `text/plain`, `multipart/*`, and `text/xml` or `application/xml`. For other mime types, that's where the `DataHandler` comes into play.

```
AttachmentPart attachment = soapMessage.createAttachmentPart();
attachment.setContent(textContent, "text/plain");
soapMessage.addAttachmentPart(attachment);
```

What you put in your SOAP message really depends upon the service you are connecting to. Just be sure to identify the destination in the `SOAPEnvelope`.

Table 7-1 includes a list of the key interfaces and classes found in the `javax.xml.soap` package.

Table 7-1. *Key SOAP Classes and Interfaces*

Name	Description
AttachmentPart	SOAPMessage attachment
Detail	DetailEntry container
DetailEntry	SOAPFault details
MessageFactory	SOAPMessage factory
MimeHeader	Mime type details
MimeHeaders	MimeHeader container
Name	XML name
Node	Element of XML document
SAAJMetaFactory	SAAJ API factory
SAAJResult	JAXP transformation or JAXB marshalling results holder
SOAPBody	SOAP body part of SOAPMessage
SOAPBodyElement	SOAPBody contents
SOAPConnection	Point-to-point connection for client
SOAPConnectionFactory	SOAPConnection factory
SOAPConstants	SOAP 1.1 protocol constants
SOAPElement	SOAPMessage element
SOAPElementFactory	SOAPElement factory
SOAPEnvelope	SOAPMessage header information
SOAPException	Standard exception for SOAP-related operations
SOAPFactory	SOAPMessage elements factory

Continued

Table 7-1. *Continued*

Name	Description
SOAPFault	SOAPMessage element for error status information
SOAPFaultElement	SOAPFault contents
SOAPHeader	SOAPMessage header element
SOAPHeaderElement	SOAPHeader contents
SOAPMessage	Base class for SOAP messages
SOAPPart	SOAPMessage element for SOAP-specific pieces
Text	Textual node contents

The contents of the SOAPMessage generated really depend upon the web service you are connecting to. Similar to how the example from Chapter 6 was built up, you just create the different elements and put the pieces together. As the javadoc for the package states, there are lots of things you can do with the javax.xml.soap package:

- Create a point-to-point connection to a specified endpoint

- Create a SOAP message

- Create an XML fragment

- Add content to the header of a SOAP message

- Add content to the body of a SOAP message

- Create attachment parts and add content to them

- Access/add/modify parts of a SOAP message

- Create/add/modify SOAP fault information

- Extract content from a SOAP message

- Send a SOAP request-response message

The JAX-WS API

The next identical packages shared with Java EE 5 are the javax.xml.ws package and subpackages, which include JAX-WS. Again, there are whole books written just about this API, so I'll just show off some highlights. Since the API is identical to that of Java EE 5, those books go into much more detail of the API than can be shown in a Mustang quick start–type book. The key difference now is that the JAX-WS libraries are standard with the Java SE platform, so no additional libraries are needed.

The key thing to understand when using the JAX-WS API with Mustang—outside the context of Java EE—is that you need to think in the context of a consumer of web services, not as a developer of them. For instance, take Google, which is a rather popular search engine. Google offers a set of web services to utilize its services from your programs. You can now use these programs directly in your program, provided you get a free key from them, which is limited to 1,000 usages a day.

Listing 7-4 provides the source for a simple web services client. Provided that you pass the file name for the SOAP request to the program, it will connect to the Google site to get results.

Listing 7-4. *Connecting to Google Web Services*

```java
import java.io.*;
import java.net.*;
import javax.xml.ws.*;
import javax.xml.namespace.*;
import javax.xml.soap.*;
public class GoogleSearch {
  public static void main(String args[]) throws Exception {
  URL url = new URL("http://api.google.com/GoogleSearch.wsdl");
  QName serviceName = new QName("urn:GoogleSearch", "GoogleSearchService");
  QName portName = new QName("urn:GoogleSearch", "GoogleSearchPort");
  Service service = Service.create(url, serviceName);
  Dispatch<SOAPMessage> dispatch = service.createDispatch(portName,
  SOAPMessage.class, Service.Mode.MESSAGE);
  SOAPMessage request = MessageFactory.newInstance().createMessage(
    null, new FileInputStream(args[0]));
  SOAPMessage response = dispatch.invoke(request);
  response.writeTo(System.out);
  }
}
```

That's a typical web services client. You can either build up the SOAP message with the previously described javax.xml.soap package, or, as the program does, just place the XML for the SOAP request in a file (with *your* Google key) as part of the SOAP message. Then, you can query Google from your program.

```
> java GoogleSearch search.xml
```

■**Note** For more information on using Google's APIs, see `www.google.com/apis`.

To change this client to use another web service, you'll need to change the URL you connect to, as well as the qualified name, `QName`, for the service. And, of course, adjust the XML of the SOAP request accordingly. Not to belittle the JAX-WS API, but that is really all there is to using the API for a client, as opposed to creating the service itself.

■**Note** Information on web services available from Amazon can be found at `http://developer.`
`amazonwebservices.com`, if you want another source to try out.

Summary

The web services support added to Mustang is meant purely for the client-side aspect of web services. There is no web server to deploy your services to. Through the three-pronged approach of JAXB, JAX-WS, and SAAJ, you can connect to any preexisting services for tasks that used to be done with RMI and CORBA, among many other pre-existing remote procedure call (RPC)–like services. The APIs themselves aren't new to the Java platform—they're just new to the standard edition.

Chapter 8 moves beyond what you can think of as standard libraries into the APIs related to directly using the platform toolset. Working with JSR 199, you can now compile your Java programs from your Java programs to create new Java programs, or at least new classes. The API even allows you to compile straight from memory, without files. Turn the page to learn about the `javax.tools` API.

CHAPTER 8

■■■

The Java Compiler API

Care to compile your source from source? Thanks to JSR 199 and the Java Compiler API, you can now initiate the standard compiler from your own code. No longer do you have to call the nonstandard Main class of the com.sun.tools.javac package to compile your code (the class/package is found in the tools.jar file in the lib subdirectory). Now you can access the compiler through the javax.tools package, without adding an extra JAR file to your classpath. As the package is brand new for Java 6, Table 8-1 shows the size of the package in the new release only.

Table 8-1. *javax.tools.* Package Size*

Package	Version	Interfaces	Classes	Enums	Total
tools	6.0	11	6	3	20

Compiling Source, Take 1

The API to compile source has a couple of different options. First, let's look at the quick-and-dirty way of compiling source. With this manner, compilation errors are sent to standard error (stderr) to be processed outside the context of the compiling program.

To invoke the Java compiler from your Java programs, you need to access the JavaCompilerTool interface. Among other things, accessing the interface allows you to set the source path, the classpath, and the destination directory. Specifying each of the files to compile as a JavaFileObject allows you to compile them all—but you're not going to need all those options just yet.

To access the default implementation of the JavaCompilerTool interface, you need to ask something called the ToolProvider. The ToolProvider class provides a getSystemJavaCompilerTool() method, which returns an instance of some class that implements the JavaCompilerTool interface.

```
JavaCompilerTool tool = ToolProvider.getSystemJavaCompilerTool();
```

■**Note** The `JavaCompilerTool` interface is not related to the `java.lang.Compiler` class, which serves as a placeholder for a just-in-time (JIT) compiler implementation.

The simple way to compile with the `JavaCompilerTool` relies on only the `Tool` interface it implements—more specifically, its `run()` method.

```
int run(InputStream in, OutputStream out, OutputStream err, String... arguments)
```

The stream arguments can all be passed in null to use the defaults of `System.in`, `System.out`, and `System.err`, respectively, for the first three arguments. The variable set of `String` arguments represents the file names to pass into the compiler. Technically speaking, you can pass any command-line arguments into `javac` here.

So, if your source code for the `Foo` class is located in the current subdirectory, the way to compile its source would be as follows:

```
int results = tool.run(null, null, null, "Foo.java");
```

There are two ways to see the results of a compilation. The first way is the obvious one: look for the necessary `.class` file in the destination directory. The third null argument passed into the `run()` method of `JavaCompilerTool` says to send output to standard error (`stderr`). This is for the compilation error messages, not just messages like those you get from not passing any files to compile to the `run()` method. The second way to check is via the returned integer. This method returns an `int` indicating success or failure of the operation. On error, you would get a nonzero value. On success, you would get a zero. The javadoc for the class gives no significance to what the non-zero error value is. If multiple source files are passed into the `run()` method, 0 will be returned only if all files compile successfully. Listing 8-1 puts all these pieces together for a first look at initiating the Java compiler from source.

Listing 8-1. *Using the Java Compiling Tool*

```
import java.io.*;
import javax.tools.*;

public class FirstCompile {
  public static void main(String args[]) throws IOException {
    JavaCompilerTool compiler = ToolProvider.getSystemJavaCompilerTool();
    int results = compiler.run(null, null, null, "Foo.java");
    System.out.println("Success: " + (results == 0));
  }
}
```

Compiling and running the program without a `Foo.java` file in the current directory will produce the following results:

```
>java FirstCompile
error: cannot read: Foo.java
1 error
Success: false
```

If instead you have the `Foo` class source defined in the current directory (as in Listing 8-2), running the program will generate a `Foo.class` file. By default, the compiled class file will be placed in the same directory as the source. On successful completion, the program displays a `Success: true` message.

Listing 8-2. *Simple Class to Compile*

```java
public class Foo {
  public static void main(String args[]) {
    System.out.println("Hello, World");
  }
}
```

To see what happens when the program to compile has an error, add a problem to the `Foo` source file, such as renaming the `println()` method to be `pritnln()`. You don't need to recompile the `FirstCompile` program; just save the updated `Foo.java` file. Then, rerunning the program gives the following output:

```
>java FirstCompile
Foo.java:3: cannot find symbol
symbol  : method pritnln(java.lang.String)
location: class java.io.PrintStream
    System.out.pritnln("Hello, World");
              ^
1 error
Success: false
```

You're seeing here exactly what `javac` spits out, since all Listing 8-1 does is use the default `stdout` and `stderr` when running the compiler.

```
javac Foo.java
Foo.java:3: cannot find symbol
symbol  : method pritnln(java.lang.String)
location: class java.io.PrintStream
    System.out.pritnln("Hello, World");
              ^
1 error
```

Compiling Source, Take 2

The FirstCompile program in Listing 8-1 shows one way of using the JavaCompilerTool class. It compiles your source files to generate .class files. For that example, all default options of the JavaCompilerTool were used for compilation—just as in doing javac Foo.java from the command line. While it certainly works, you can do a little more work up front to generate better results, or at least a potentially better user experience.

Introducing StandardJavaFileManager

The "Compiling Source, Take 1" section took the easy way out to compile source code. Yes, it worked, but it didn't really offer a way to see or do much with the results from within the program, short of reading standard error/output, that is. The better approach at compiling source from source is to take advantage of the StandardJavaFileManager class. The file manager provides a way to work with regular files for both input and output operations, and to get diagnostic messages reported through the help of a DiagnosticListener. The DiagnosticCollector class is just one such implementation of that listener that you'll be using.

Before identifying what needs to be compiled, the basic two-step process to get the file manager is to create a DiagnosticCollector and then ask the JavaCompilerTool for the file manager with getStandardFileManager(), passing in DiagnosticListener. This listener reports non-fatal problems and can be shared with the compiler by passing it into the getTask() method.

```
DiagnosticCollector<JavaFileObject> diagnostics =
    new DiagnosticCollector<JavaFileObject>();
StandardJavaFileManager fileManager =
    compiler.getStandardFileManager(diagnostics);
```

Providing a null listener works, but that puts you back to where you were before, without a way to monitor diagnostic messages. I'll discuss more on DiagnosticCollector and DiagnosticListener later, though.

Before getting into the depths of StandardJavaFileManager, I want to discuss the getTask() method of the JavaCompilerTool class, an important part of the compilation process. It takes six arguments and passes back an instance of an inner class of itself, called CompilationTask.

```
JavaCompilerTool.CompilationTask getTask(
  Writer out,
  JavaFileManager fileManager,
  DiagnosticListener<? super JavaFileObject> diagnosticListener,
  Iterable<String> options,
  Iterable<String> classes,
  Iterable<? extends JavaFileObject> compilationUnits)
```

Most of these arguments can be null, with logical defaults.

- out: System.err

- fileManager: The compiler's standard file manager

- diagnosticListener: The compiler's default behavior

- options: No command-line options given to the compiler

- classes: No class names provided for annotation processing

The last argument, compilationUnits, really shouldn't be null, as that is what you want to compile. And that brings us back to StandardJavaFileManager. Notice the argument type: Iterable<? extends JavaFileObject>. There are two methods of StandardJavaFileManager that give you these results. You can either start with a List of File objects, or a List of String objects, representing the file names.

```
Iterable<? extends JavaFileObject> getJavaFileObjectsFromFiles(
    Iterable<? extends File> files)
Iterable<? extends JavaFileObject> getJavaFileObjectsFromStrings(
    Iterable<String> names)
```

Actually, anything that implements Iterable can be used to identify the collection of items to compile here—not just a List—it just happens to be the easiest to create.

```
String[] filenames = ...;
Iterable<? extends JavaFileObject> compilationUnits =
    fileManager.getJavaFileObjectsFromFiles(Arrays.asList(filenames));
```

You now have all the bits to do the actual compilation of your source files. The `JavaCompilerTool.CompilationTask` returned from `getTask()` implements `Runnable`. You can either pass it off to a `Thread` to execute separately or call the `run()` method directly for synchronous execution.

```
JavaCompilerTool.CompilationTask task =
    compiler.getTask(null, fileManager, null, null, null, compilationUnits);
task.run();
```

Assuming there are no compilation warnings or errors, you'll get all the files identified by the `compilationUnits` variable compiled (and their dependencies). To find out if everything succeeded, call the `getResult()` method of `CompilationTask`. This returns `true` if all the compilation units compiled without errors, and `false` if one or more fail.

As a last task, remember to release the resources of the file manager with its `close()` method. You can call `getTask()` multiple times to reuse the compiler, in order to reduce any overhead during multiple compilation requests. Just close things up when you're done.

```
fileManager.close();
```

Putting all the pieces together and doing nothing special with the `DiagnosticListener/DiagnosticCollector` produces Listing 8-3. If you're following the source examples in the book, don't forget to rename the `pritnln()` method to be `println()` again.

Listing 8-3. *More Advanced Compilation Options*

```
import java.io.*;
import java.util.*;
import javax.tools.*;

public class SecondCompile {
  public static void main(String args[]) throws IOException {
    JavaCompilerTool compiler = ToolProvider.getSystemJavaCompilerTool();
    DiagnosticCollector<JavaFileObject> diagnostics =
        new DiagnosticCollector<JavaFileObject>();
    StandardJavaFileManager fileManager =
        compiler.getStandardFileManager(diagnostics);
    Iterable<? extends JavaFileObject> compilationUnits =
        fileManager.getJavaFileObjectsFromStrings(Arrays.asList("Foo.java"));
    JavaCompilerTool.CompilationTask task = compiler.getTask(
        null, fileManager, diagnostic, null, null, compilationUnits);
    task.run();
    boolean success = task.getResult();
```

```
    fileManager.close();
    System.out.println("Success: " + success);
  }
}
```

Assuming there are no compilation errors, compiling and running the program in Listing 8-3 produces the following output and a compiled Foo class:

```
java SecondCompile
Success: true
```

With a compilation error, you would see false there, instead of true, but no diagnostics about the problems—which takes us to DiagnosticListener and its DiagnosticCollector implementation.

Working with DiagnosticListener

Compilation errors are reported to the registered DiagnosticListener. The DiagnosticListener interface has a single method, public void report(Diagnostic<? extends S> diagnostic), which you must implement. Actually, you don't have to implement it yourself. The standard libraries offer one such implementation in the DiagnosticCollector class. As the name implies, the DiagnosticCollector class collects the diagnostic problems it encounters. You can then loop through the information with a simple enhanced for loop.

```
for (Diagnostic diagnostic : diagnostics.getDiagnostics())
    System.console().printf(
        "Code: %s%n" +
        "Kind: %s%n" +
        "Position: %s%n" +
        "Start Position: %s%n" +
        "End Position: %s%n" +
        "Source: %s%n" +
        "Message:  %s%n",
        diagnostic.getCode(), diagnostic.getKind(),
        diagnostic.getPosition(), diagnostic.getStartPosition(),
        diagnostic.getEndPosition(), diagnostic.getSource(),
        diagnostic.getMessage(null));
```

Of course, if you want to create your own DiagnosticListener, you can do that, too. As previously mentioned, it gets a Diagnostic passed into its report() method, too.

Changing the Output Directory

One of the typical things developers do is maintain separate source and destination directories, into which the source and the compiled .class files are respectively placed. The JavaCompilerTool class supports this by setting the output directory via the options argument passed into its getTask() method. Configuring the compilation task appropriately will tell the tool to place the compiled class files into a different location than the source files.

```
Iterable<String> options = Arrays.asList("-d", "classes");
JavaCompilerTool.CompilationTask task = compiler.getTask(
    null, fileManager, diagnostics, options, null, compilationUnits);
```

As it probably appears, you're just configuring the command-line options, just as if you used the -d command-line switch with the javac compiler.

Changing the Input Directory

The JavaFileObject class is used to identify each source file to compile. You provide the file name as a string to the getJavaFileObjectsFromStrings() method, or as a File to the getJavaFileObjectsFromFiles() method of your StandardJavaFileManager. For instance, "Foo.java" would be used to compile the Foo class located in the default package. As soon as the source code belongs to a package, you then maintain that package structure within the argument of the getJavaFileObjectsFromStrings() method call. For instance, had the Foo class been in the com.example package, the argument to getJavaFileObjectsFromStrings() would have been "com/example/Foo.java" instead.

■Tip Even on Windows platforms, the path elements should be separated by Unix-style file separators.

If compiling one class reveals that a second class needs to be compiled, where does the system look for it? By default, it looks in the current directory, or at least relative to the top-level package directory when in a package.

From the command-line compiler, you can provide an additional set of locations for the compiler to look, via the -sourcepath option. With the JavaCompilerTool class, you just need to add more options for the getTask() method to identify those locations.

```
Iterable<String> options = Arrays.asList("-d", "classes", "-sourcepath", "src");
```

This doesn't help in locating the actual JavaFileObject being compiled, only in finding the source files for its dependent classes.

To demonstrate these new options, Listings 8-4 and 8-5 provide two classes to use. Place the Bar class of Listing 8-4 in the current directory, and the Baz class of Listing 8-5 in a subdirectory named src.

Listing 8-4. *Simple Class to Compile with Dependency*

```
import java.util.*;

public class Bar {
  public static void main(String args[]) {
    System.out.println("Move that Bus");
    new Baz();
    List list = new ArrayList();
    list.add("Hello");
    new Thread().suspend();
  }
}
```

Listing 8-5. *Dependent Class to Compile*

```
public class Baz {
}
```

Before creating a new program to compile this with JSR 199 and the Java Compiler API, it is important to see what happens when you compile with javac and the extended lint option enabled.

```
> javac -d classes -sourcepath src -Xlint:all Bar.java
Bar.java:8: warning: [unchecked] unchecked call to add(E) as a member of the raw
 type java.util.List
    list.add("Hello");
        ^
Bar.java:9: warning: [deprecation] suspend() in java.lang.Thread has been
deprecated
    new Thread().suspend();
             ^
2 warnings
```

In the first case, the usage of the List object does not properly identify that it is a list of String objects via generics, so the compiler issues a warning. In the latter case, the suspend() method of Thread has been deprecated, so it shouldn't be used.

■**Note** At this point, you should delete the generated .class files for both the Bar and Baz classes.

Listing 8-6 puts all these pieces of JavaCompilerTool together with its DiagnosticCollector and changes to the default source and destination directories. Be sure to change the file to be compiled from Foo.java to Bar.java. Along with the new output from the DiagnosticCollection, the three bold source lines are the ones that changed from the earlier example.

Listing 8-6. *Compiling with a DiagnosticListener*

```
import java.io.*;
import java.util.*;
import javax.tools.*;

public class SecondCompile {
  public static void main(String args[]) throws IOException {
    JavaCompilerTool compiler = ToolProvider.getSystemJavaCompilerTool();
    DiagnosticCollector<JavaFileObject> diagnostics =
        new DiagnosticCollector<JavaFileObject>();
    StandardJavaFileManager fileManager =
        compiler.getStandardFileManager(diagnostics);
    Iterable<? extends JavaFileObject> compilationUnits =
        fileManager.getJavaFileObjectsFromStrings(Arrays.asList("Bar.java"));
    Iterable<String> options = Arrays.asList(
        "-d", "classes", "-sourcepath", "src");
    JavaCompilerTool.CompilationTask task = compiler.getTask(
        null, fileManager, diagnostics, options, null, compilationUnits);
    task.run();
    boolean success = task.getResult();
    for (Diagnostic diagnostic : diagnostics.getDiagnostics())
        System.console().printf(
            "Code: %s%n" +
            "Kind: %s%n" +
            "Position: %s%n" +
            "Start Position: %s%n" +
            "End Position: %s%n" +
```

```
            "Source: %s%n" +
            "Message:  %s%n",
            diagnostic.getCode(), diagnostic.getKind(),
            diagnostic.getPosition(), diagnostic.getStartPosition(),
            diagnostic.getEndPosition(), diagnostic.getSource(),
            diagnostic.getMessage(null));
      fileManager.close();
      System.out.println("Success: " + success);
    }
}
```

After compiling SecondCompile, running the program will generate .class files for the Bar and Baz classes in the classes subdirectory. It will also display information from the Diagnostic of the warning messages, as shown here:

```
> java SecondCompile
Code: compiler.note.deprecated.filename
Kind: NOTE
Position: -1
Start Position: -1
End Position: -1
Source: null
Message:  Note: Bar.java uses or overrides a deprecated API.
Code: compiler.note.deprecated.recompile
Kind: NOTE
Position: -1
Start Position: -1
End Position: -1
Source: null
Message:  Note: Recompile with -Xlint:deprecation for details.
Code: compiler.note.unchecked.filename
Kind: NOTE
Position: -1
Start Position: -1
End Position: -1
Source: null
Message:  Note: Bar.java uses unchecked or unsafe operations.
Code: compiler.note.unchecked.recompile
Kind: NOTE
Position: -1
Start Position: -1
End Position: -1
```

```
Source: null
Message:  Note: Recompile with -Xlint:unchecked for details.
Success: true
```

Compiling from Memory

My favorite use of JavaCompilerTool isn't just compiling source files found on disk. The class also allows you to generate files in memory, compile them, and then, using reflection, run them. The javadoc for the JavaCompilerTool interface defines a JavaSourceFromString class that makes this so much easier. Basically, the JavaSourceFromString class is a JavaFileObject that defines an in-memory source file. Once created, you can then pass it on to the compiler to define a CompilationTask. You can then compile that source directly using the same run() call as before, to get a generated .class file. Compiling source from memory sounds like a lot of work, but as Listing 8-7 shows, it isn't really that hard at all. The in-memory class definition is shown in bold. While the compiler doesn't care about whitespace, it is best to format the source in a logical way for readability's sake. The definition of the JavaSourceFromString class follows in Listing 8-8. The source file is literally in-memory only, without anything stored to disk.

Listing 8-7. *Compiling from Memory*

```
import java.lang.reflect.*;
import java.io.*;
import javax.tools.*;
import javax.tools.JavaCompilerTool.CompilationTask;
import java.util.*;

public class CompileSource {
  public static void main(String args[]) throws IOException {
    JavaCompilerTool compiler = ToolProvider.getSystemJavaCompilerTool();
    DiagnosticCollector<JavaFileObject> diagnostics =
        new DiagnosticCollector<JavaFileObject>();

    // Define class
    StringWriter writer = new StringWriter();
    PrintWriter out = new PrintWriter(writer);
    out.println("public class HelloWorld {");
    out.println("  public static void main(String args[]) {");
    out.println("    System.out.println(\"Hello, World\");");
```

```
out.println("   }");
out.println("}");
out.close();
JavaFileObject file =
  new JavaSourceFromString("HelloWorld", writer.toString());

// Compile class
Iterable<? extends JavaFileObject> compilationUnits =
    Arrays.asList(file);
CompilationTask task = compiler.getTask(
    null, null, diagnostics, null, null, compilationUnits);
task.run();
boolean success = task.getResult();
for (Diagnostic diagnostic : diagnostics.getDiagnostics())
    System.console().printf(
        "Code: %s%n" +
        "Kind: %s%n" +
        "Position: %s%n" +
        "Start Position: %s%n" +
        "End Position: %s%n" +
        "Source: %s%n" +
        "Message:  %s%n",
        diagnostic.getCode(), diagnostic.getKind(),
        diagnostic.getPosition(), diagnostic.getStartPosition(),
        diagnostic.getEndPosition(), diagnostic.getSource(),
        diagnostic.getMessage(null));
System.out.println("Success: " + success);

// Invoke new class
if (success) {
  try {
    System.out.println("-----Output-----");
    Class.forName("HelloWorld").getDeclaredMethod("main",
      new Class[] {String[].class}).invoke(null, new Object[] {null});
    System.out.println("-----Output-----");
  } catch (ClassNotFoundException e) {
    System.err.println("Class not found: " + e);
  } catch (NoSuchMethodException e) {
    System.err.println("No such method: " + e);
  } catch (IllegalAccessException e) {
    System.err.println("Illegal access: " + e);
  } catch (InvocationTargetException e) {
```

```
        System.err.println("Invocation target: " + e);
      }
    }
  }
}
```

Listing 8-8. *The JavaSourceFromString Class Definition*

```
import javax.tools.*;
import java.net.*;

public class JavaSourceFromString extends SimpleJavaFileObject {
  final String code;

  JavaSourceFromString(String name, String code) {
    super(URI.create(
      "string:///" + name.replace('.','/') + Kind.SOURCE.extension),
      Kind.SOURCE);
    this.code = code;
  }

  @Override
  public CharSequence getCharContent(boolean ignoreEncodingErrors) {
    return code;
  }
}
```

Running the `CompileSource` program generates the following output:

```
> java CompileSource
Success: true
-----Output-----
Hello, World
-----Output-----
```

Summary

The Java Compiler API isn't needed by everyone. In fact, it isn't needed by most people. It's great for those creating tools like editors, or something like JSP engines, which require real-time compilation. Thanks to JSR 199, you can do this with Java 6.

Chapter 9 moves on to JSR 223, which incorporates even more new features into Mustang. This JSR defines a framework for combining the scripting world with the Java world, enabling scripting languages to interact with full-fledged Java objects in a standard way. No longer will you have to explore any vendor-specific options, thanks to the new `javax.script` and `javax.script.http` packages.

CHAPTER 9

■ ■ ■

Scripting and JSR 223

What can it be now? When I first heard about scripting support in Java 6, I understood it to mean that the Mozilla Rhino JavaScript interpreter would be embedded in the platform. Using a JEditorPane, you would be able to not only show HTML in the component, but also have it execute the JavaScript on the web pages your users visit, allowing the component to be more like a full-fledged browser than just an HTML viewer for help text. But, that isn't where the scripting support in Mustang went. Instead, while Rhino is present, JSR 223 adds to Mustang a common interface to integrate any scripting language (like PHP or Ruby—not just JavaScript), a framework for those scripting languages to access the Java platform, and a command-line scripting shell program, jrunscript.

Before looking at the different elements offered by JSR 223, take a look at Table 9-1, which shows the relatively small size of the javax.script package, which provides the public APIs to the new scripting support library.

Table 9-1. *javax.script.* Package Sizes*

Package	Version	Interfaces	Classes	Throwable	Total
script	6.0	6	5	0+1	12

While I haven't been involved with JSR 223 since its beginning in 2003, I've gathered that the JSR originated from a desire for a language for scripting web servlets with something comparable to the Bean Scripting Framework (or BSF for short). Yes, BSF is an Apache project (see http://jakarta.apache.org/bsf). BSF offered (offers?) a tag library for JavaServer Pages (JSP), allowing you to write web pages in languages other than the Java programming language. A package named something like javax.script.http would integrate with your servlets for execution on your web servers, with the script results passed back to the browser.

At least for Mustang, what seems to have morphed out of the deal is something more appropriate for the standard edition of Java than for the enterprise edition. So, instead of a new javax.script.http package, you get just javax.script with no real direct web hooks, yet. And as best as can be found, it has little to no direct servlet or JSP relationship. Surely the framework is there for tighter enterprise integration; it is just that Mustang only requires Mustang to run its classes, not some enterprise edition of the Java platform. At least with Mustang, you won't find any servlet objects related to JSR 223.

Scripting Engines

The scripting package added with Mustang is rather small, at least from the public API perspective: six interfaces, five classes, and an exception. Looking behind the scenes, though, there are many nonpublic elements involved. For instance, the embedded Rhino JavaScript engine has over 140 classes—you just never see them or know that you're working with them, thanks to those six interfaces that are defined in the javax.script package. What you'll learn here is how to use the interfaces, not how to create your own engine.

The main class of the javax.script package is called ScriptEngineManager. The class provides a discovery mechanism to the installed ScriptEngineFactory objects, which in turn provide access to an actual ScriptEngine. Listing 9-1 demonstrates this relationship from ScriptEngineManager to ScriptEngineFactory to ScriptEngine, displaying information about each factory found. Nothing is actually done with the engine just yet.

Listing 9-1. *Listing Available Scripting Engine Factories*

```
import javax.script.*;
import java.io.*;
import java.util.*;

public class ListEngines {
  public static void main(String args[]) {
    ScriptEngineManager manager = new ScriptEngineManager();
    List<ScriptEngineFactory> factories = manager.getEngineFactories();
    for (ScriptEngineFactory factory: factories) {
      Console console = System.console();
      console.printf("Name: %s%n" +
                     "Version: %s%n" +
                     "Language name: %s%n" +
                     "Language version: %s%n" +
                     "Extensions: %s%n" +
                     "Mime types: %s%n" +
                     "Names: %s%n",
                     factory.getEngineName(),
                     factory.getEngineVersion(),
                     factory.getLanguageName(),
```

```
                    factory.getLanguageVersion(),
                    factory.getExtensions(),
                    factory.getMimeTypes(),
                    factory.getNames());
      ScriptEngine engine = factory.getScriptEngine();
    }
  }
}
```

Running the program demonstrates that the only installed engine is version 1.6, release 2, of the Mozilla Rhino engine.

```
> java ListEngines
Name: Mozilla Rhino
Version: 1.6 release 2
Language name: ECMAScript
Language version: 1.6
Extensions: [js]
Mime types: [application/javascript, application/ecmascript, text/javascript,
   text/ecmascript]
Names: [js, rhino, JavaScript, javascript, ECMAScript, ecmascript]
```

The last line represents the different names that can be used to locate this engine from the manager.

While getting the scripting engine from the factory that was acquired from the scripting manager certainly works, you don't need to go through that level of indirection. Instead, you can ask the manager directly for the engine associated with a particular extension, mime type, or name, as follows:

```
ScriptEngine engine1 = manager.getEngineByExtension("js");
ScriptEngine engine2 = manager.getEngineByMimeType("text/javascript");
ScriptEngine engine3 = manager.getEngineByName("javascript");
```

The getEngineByXXX() methods are not static methods of ScriptEngineManager, so you have to create an instance first; but if you know you want to evaluate a JavaScript expression, just ask for the JavaScript engine, and then use the returned engine to evaluate the expression.

Note There are two constructors for ScriptEngineManager, with a class loader passed into one, allowing you to provide multiple contexts for where to locate additional engines.

To have a scripting engine evaluate an expression, you would use one of the six versions of its eval() method, all of which can throw a ScriptException if there are errors in the script:

- public Object eval(String script)

- public Object eval(Reader reader)

- public Object eval(String script, ScriptContext context)

- public Object eval(Reader reader, ScriptContext context)

- public Object eval(String script, Bindings bindings)

- public Object eval(Reader reader, Bindings bindings)

The script to evaluate can either be in the form of a String object or come from a Reader stream. The ScriptContext allows you to specify the scope of any Bindings objects, as well as get input, output, and error streams. There are two predefined context scopes: ScriptContext.GLOBAL_SCOPE and ScriptContext.ENGINE_SCOPE. The Bindings objects are just a mapping from a String name to a Java instance, with *global scope* meaning that names are shared across all engines.

■**Tip** To set the default context for an engine, for when a ScriptContext isn't passed into eval(), call the setContext() method of ScriptEngine.

Listing 9-2 demonstrates the evaluation of a simple JavaScript expression from a string. It gets the current hour and displays an appropriate message. The JavaScript code itself is in bold.

Listing 9-2. *Evaluating JavaScript*

```
import javax.script.*;
import java.io.*;

public class RunJavaScript {
  public static void main(String args[]) {
    ScriptEngineManager manager = new ScriptEngineManager();
    ScriptEngine engine = manager.getEngineByName("javascript");
    try {
      Double hour = (Double)engine.eval(
```

```
      "var date = new Date();" +
      "date.getHours();");
    String msg;
    if (hour < 10) {
      msg = "Good morning";
    } else if (hour < 16) {
      msg = "Good afternoon";
    } else if (hour < 20) {
      msg = "Good evening";
    } else {
      msg = "Good night";
    }
    Console console = System.console();
    console.printf("Hour %s: %s%n", hour, msg);
  } catch (ScriptException e) {
    System.err.println(e);
  }
 }
}
```

Depending upon the current time of day, you'll get different results.

```
> java RunJavaScript
Hour 8.0: Good morning
```

The last thing to really demonstrate in the API here is Bindings. First off is the primary reason to use Bindings: they offer the means of passing Java objects into the scripting world. While you can certainly get the Bindings object for a ScriptEngine and work with it as a Map, the ScriptEngine interface has get() and put() methods that work directly with the bindings of the engine.

The FlipBindings class in Listing 9-3 shows the indirect use of the Bindings class. The program accepts a single command-line argument, which is passed into the JavaScript engine via a binding. In turn, the JavaScript reverses the string and passes the results out as a different binding. The reversed string is then displayed to the user.

Listing 9-3. *Reversing a String Through ScriptEngine Bindings*

```
import javax.script.*;
import java.io.*;
```

```java
public class FlipBindings {
  public static void main(String args[]) {
    ScriptEngineManager manager = new ScriptEngineManager();
    ScriptEngine engine = manager.getEngineByName("javascript");
    if (args.length != 1) {
      System.err.println("Please pass name on command line");
      System.exit(-1);
    }

    try {
      engine.put("name", args[0]);
      engine.eval(
        "var output = '';" +
        "for (i = 0; i <= name.length; i++) {" +
        "  output = name.charAt(i) + output" +
        "}");
      String name = (String)engine.get("output");
      Console console = System.console();
      console.printf("Reversed: %s%n", name);
    } catch (ScriptException e) {
      System.err.println(e);
    }
  }
}
```

Passing in the book name to the program shows the reversed title:

```
> java FlipBindings "Java 6 Platform Revealed"
Reversed: delaeveR mroftalP 6 avaJ
```

■**Note** Errors in the JavaScript source are handled by the caught `ScriptException`. It is best to at least print out this exception, as it will reveal errors in the script code. You can also get the file name, line number, and column number in which the error happened.

The Compilable Interface

Typically, scripting languages are interpreted. What this means is that each time the scripting source is read, it is evaluated before executing. To optimize execution time, you can compile some of that source such that future executions are faster. That is where the Compilable interface comes into play. If a specific scripting engine also implements Compilable, then you can precompile scripts before execution. The compilation process involves the compile() method of Compilable, and returns a CompiledScript upon success. As shown in Listing 9-4, execution of the compiled script is now done with the eval() method of CompiledScript, instead of the ScriptEngine.

Listing 9-4. *Working with Compilable Scripts*

```
import javax.script.*;
import java.io.*;

public class CompileTest {
  public static void main(String args[]) {
    ScriptEngineManager manager = new ScriptEngineManager();
    ScriptEngine engine = manager.getEngineByName("javascript");
    engine.put("counter", 0);
    if (engine instanceof Compilable) {
      Compilable compEngine = (Compilable)engine;
      try {
        CompiledScript script = compEngine.compile(
          "function count() { " +
          "  counter = counter +1; " +
          "  return counter; " +
          "}; count();");
        Console console = System.console();
        console.printf("Counter: %s%n", script.eval());
        console.printf("Counter: %s%n", script.eval());
        console.printf("Counter: %s%n", script.eval());
      } catch (ScriptException e) {
        System.err.println(e);
      }
    } else {
      System.err.println("Engine can't compile code");
    }
  }
}
```

The CompileTest example here just adds 1 to a counter variable stored in the bindings of the ScriptEngine. Since the script is evaluated three times, its final value is 3.

```
> java CompileTest
Counter: 1.0
Counter: 2.0
Counter: 3.0
```

Compiling scripts can also be done from files, or more specifically, from Reader strings. Compilation is most beneficial for both large code blocks and those that execute repeatedly.

The Invocable Interface

Invocable is another optional interface that a scripting engine can implement. An invocable engine supports the calling of functions scripted in that engine's language. Not only can you call functions directly, but you can also bind functions of the scripting language to interfaces in Java space.

Once a method/function has been evaluated by the engine, it can be invoked via the invoke() method of Invocable—assuming of course that the engine implements the interface. Invocable functions can also be passed parameters that don't have to come through bindings; just pass in the method name to be executed and its arguments. To demonstrate, Listing 9-5 takes the earlier string reversal example from Listing 9-3 and makes the reversal code an invocable function.

Listing 9-5. *Using Invocable to Reverse Strings*

```
import javax.script.*;
import java.io.*;

public class InvocableTest {
  public static void main(String args[]) {
    ScriptEngineManager manager = new ScriptEngineManager();
    ScriptEngine engine = manager.getEngineByName("javascript");
    if (args.length == 0) {
      System.err.println("Please pass name(s) on command line");
      System.exit(-1);
    }
```

```
    try {
      engine.eval(
        "function reverse(name) {" +
        "  var output = '';" +
        "  for (i = 0; i <= name.length; i++) {" +
        "    output = name.charAt(i) + output" +
        "  }" +
        "  return output;" +
        "}");
      Invocable invokeEngine = (Invocable)engine;
      Console console = System.console();
      for (Object name: args) {
        Object o = invokeEngine.invoke("reverse", name);
        console.printf("%s / %s%n", name, o);
      }
    } catch (NoSuchMethodException e) {
      System.err.println(e);
    } catch (ScriptException e) {
      System.err.println(e);
    }
  }
}
```

Running this program involves passing multiple strings via the command-line arguments. Each one passed along the command line will be displayed in both a forward and backward fashion.

```
> java InvocableTest one two three
one / eno
two / owt
three / eerht
```

Caution There are two invoke() methods of Invocable. Sometimes the arguments can be ambiguous, and the compiler can't determine which of the two methods to use, as they both accept a variable number of arguments. In Listing 9-5, the enhanced for loop said each element was an Object, even though we knew it to be a String. This was to appease the compiler without adding a casting operation.

By itself, this doesn't make Invocable that great of an operation—but it has a second side: its getInterface() method. With the getInterface() method, you can dynamically create new implementations of interfaces by defining the implementations of an interface's methods in the scripting language.

Let's take this one a little more slowly by looking at a specific interface. The Runnable interface has one method: run(). If your scripting language has made a run() method invocable, you can acquire an instance of the Runnable interface from the Invocable engine.

First, evaluate a no-argument run() method to make it invocable:

```
engine.eval("function run() {print('wave');}");
```

Next, associate it to an instance of the interface:

```
Runnable runner = invokeEngine.getInterface(Runnable.class);
```

You can now pass this Runnable object to a Thread constructor for execution:

```
Thread t = new Thread(runner);
t.start();
```

Listing 9-6 puts all these pieces together. There is an added Thread.join() call to ensure that the newly created thread finishes before the program exits.

Listing 9-6. *Using Invocable to Implement Interfaces*

```
import javax.script.*;

public class InterfaceTest {
  public static void main(String args[]) {
    ScriptEngineManager manager = new ScriptEngineManager();
    ScriptEngine engine = manager.getEngineByName("javascript");
    try {
      engine.eval("function run() {print('wave');}");
      Invocable invokeEngine = (Invocable)engine;
      Runnable runner = invokeEngine.getInterface(Runnable.class);
      Thread t = new Thread(runner);
      t.start();
      t.join();
    } catch (InterruptedException e) {
```

```
      System.err.println(e);
    } catch (ScriptException e) {
      System.err.println(e);
    }
  }
}
```

Running the program just displays the string sent to the JavaScript `print()` method.

```
> java InterfaceTest
wave
```

---

jrunscript

Mustang includes some new programs in the `bin` directory of the JDK. Many of these are considered experimental, at least in the beta release. One such program is `jrunscript`. Think of it as command-line access to the installed scripting engines. You can try out anything with `jrunscript` that you would pass into the `eval()` method of a `ScriptEngine`.

First, to see what engines are installed, you can pass a `-q` option to `jrunscript`:

```
jrunscript -q
Language ECMAScript 1.6 implemention "Mozilla Rhino" 1.6 release 2
```

■**Tip** To see all the available commands from `jrunscript`, use the `-?` or `-help` command-line options.

With only one available in the default installation from Sun, you don't have to explicitly request to use a specific engine. But, if multiple were available, you could explicitly request a language with the `-l` option. The language string to pass in would be one of those returned from the scripting engine factory's `getNames()` method. As Listing 9-1 showed, any of the following will work for the provided ECMAScript 1.6 engine: `js`, `rhino`, `JavaScript`, `javascript`, `ECMAScript`, or `ecmascript`. Yes, the names are case sensitive.

```
> jrunscript -l javascripT
script engine for language javascripT can not be found
```

Assuming you start with a matching language, you are then in interactive mode with the script runner.

```
> jrunscript
js>
```

Just enter your JavaScript interactively and it will be evaluated. You can also have the tool evaluate whole files by using the -f option from the command line.

Get Your Pnuts Here

JavaScript isn't the only scripting engine available, just the only one that ships with Mustang. Pronounced like *peanuts*, Pnuts is another engine that works with JSR 223. It's available from https://pnuts.dev.java.net. You can find configuration information at http://pnuts.org/snapshot/latest/extensions/jsr223/doc/index.html.

Hopefully, by the time Mustang ships, other scripting languages, such as Ruby or PHP, will be available in a JSR 223 installable configuration.

Note JSR 274 is about the BeanShell scripting language. It's not part of Mustang, but supposedly works alongside JSR 223. The Groovy programming language is JSR 241. It's not part of Mustang, either.

Summary

From what appears to be a long way from where JSR 223 started, Mustang gets a common scripting framework for integrating scripting engines with the Java platform. From evaluating the scripting source, to compiling and invoking, your Java programs can be bilingual with full object transparency between the two languages. In fact, you can even implement interfaces on the fly in the scripting language if you want to, without even generating .class files. As you get started with scripting, be sure to test your scripts in the command-line support tool.

The book's final chapter looks at the last big additions to Mustang—improvements in the pluggable annotation processing area. First introduced with Java 1.5, the metadata facility allows the marking of attributes for classes, interfaces, fields, and methods. In Chapter 10, you'll discover the additional features available for the processing of your types and elements.

CHAPTER 10

■ ■ ■

Pluggable Annotation Processing Updates

Are you apt to use the apt tool? Annotations are a concept introduced with the 5.0 release of J2SE and JSR 175. In this chapter, you'll explore those annotations added to Java SE 6. Although this is a Java 6 book, since annotations are so new, it is best to start with a description of what exactly they are and how to use them, and not just focus on the new ones.

Confused yet? First, apt stands for the annotation processing tool. It is a new command-line tool that comes with the JDK. (Well, it was new for the 5.0 release.) You use annotations to annotate your source code, and apt to make new annotations. Annotations are @ tags that appear in source, not javadoc-style comments. They have corresponding classes in the system, either as part of the core libraries or created by you. For instance, the @deprecated javadoc tag can be thought of as an annotation, although it isn't exactly. It acts as metadata that affects how tools and libraries interact with your classes. The @deprecated tag tells the compiler to generate a compilation warning when you use the method or class.

Before digging too deeply into annotations, though, it is important to repeat a line from the Java documentation: "Typical application programmers will never have to define an annotation type" (see http://java.sun.com/j2se/1.5.0/docs/guide/language/annotations.html). However, defining annotations is different than using them. So, let's look at using a few first.

Before going into the specifics of what to do with annotations, here's what an annotation declaration looks like:

```
package java.lang;

import java.lang.annotation.*;

@Documented
@Retention(RetentionPolicy.RUNTIME)
public @interface Deprecated {
}
```

That is the whole annotation declaration; it is like a class definition. It is for the pre-defined annotation Deprecated, to be described shortly.

JDK 5.0 Annotations

JDK 5.0 introduces three annotations: @Deprecated, @SuppressWarnings, and @Override. Let's take a quick look at what was available to us before Java SE 6.0.

The @Deprecated Annotation

One of the JDK 5.0 annotations is @Deprecated. Notice the difference in case. It is different from the javadoc @deprecated tag, as it doesn't go in javadoc comments. Instead, you place @Deprecated above the method or class you want to flag as out of date. The positioning of both tags is shown in Listing 10-1.

Listing 10-1. *@Deprecated Annotation Usage*

```
public class Dep {
  /**
   * @deprecated Don't use this method any more.
   */
  @Deprecated
  public static void myDeprecatedMethod() {
    System.out.println("Why did you do that?");
  }
}
class DeprecatedUsage {
  public void useDeprecatedMethod() {
    Dep.myDeprecatedMethod();
  }
}
```

There is a second class in Listing 10-1 that uses the deprecated method: DeprecatedUsage. When you compile the source code with the javac compiler, you get a warning:

```
> javac Dep.java
```

```
Note: Dep.java uses or overrides a deprecated API.
Note: Recompile with -Xlint:deprecation for details.
```

Then, compiling with the specified -Xlint option shows the details:

```
> javac -Xlint:deprecation Dep.java

Dep.java:11: warning: [deprecation] myDeprecatedMethod() in Dep has been deprecated
    Dep.myDeprecatedMethod();
      ^
1 warning
```

Nothing new here. This is the JDK 5.0 @Deprecate annotation—just another way of doing what @deprecated does.

The @SuppressWarnings Annotation

There are two types of annotations: those that accept arguments and those that don't. The @Deprecated annotation is an example of one that doesn't. The @SuppressWarnings annotation is one that does. With the @Deprecated annotation, a method or class is either deprecated or it isn't. Adding the metadata is an on/off flag. On the other hand, the @SuppressWarnings annotation says you would like to either suppress a specific type of warning or not. The types will be specific to the compiler vendor. For Sun's compiler, there are two warnings that can be suppressed: deprecation and unchecked. An unchecked value has to do with compile-time checks for generics. If you don't want to update legacy code to avoid warnings related to generics, you can add an @SuppressWarnings annotation to your source:

```
@SuppressWarnings({"unchecked"})
```

■**Note** You can add the suppression at the class or method level. If at the class level, all warnings of unchecked usages in the class will be suppressed.

The argument to the annotation is an array of strings—hence the extra set of {}s in there. If instead of suppressing warnings related to generics you want to avoid the warning generated by compiling the source in Listing 10-1, you would add an @SuppressWarnings({"deprecation"}) annotation to where the deprecated method call was made. Listing 10-2 shows an updated DeprecatedUsage class.

Listing 10-2. *@SuppressWarnings Annotation Usage*

```
class DeprecatedUsage {
  @SuppressWarnings("deprecation")
  public void useDeprecatedMethod() {
    Dep.myDeprecatedMethod();
  }
}
```

After adding the annotation, the compiler won't complain anymore.

The @Override Annotation

The third JDK 5.0 annotation is @Override. Use of this annotation tells the compiler that the method is supposed to be overriding a method in the superclass. The compiler will warn you if it doesn't. This will catch common mistakes, such as a method with the wrong case—for example, hashcode() versus hashCode(). In such a case, a quick scan through the code may look right, and the compiler won't complain at compilation time. Only after your resultant program produces odd results when hashCode() should be called does the problem of the incorrect case in your method reveal itself. Well, it doesn't exactly reveal itself, but you know something is wrong, and you have to hunt down the problem. By using the annotation, errors of this nature will be caught much sooner in the development process.

Listing 10-3 shows a program with a poorly overridden method.

Listing 10-3. *@Override Annotation Usage*

```
public class Over {
  public void overrideMe() {
  }
}
class SubOver extends Over {
  @Override
  public void overrideme() {
  }
}
```

Notice the poorly capitalized method without camelcase for the *m* in me. Had the source code not included the @Override annotation, the compiler would not have complained, producing a SubOver class with an overrideme() method. Any call to the overrideMe() method of SubOver would then result in the version in the parent class being called instead.

However, because of the @Override, you learn at compile time that there are problems, as shown in the following snippet:

```
> javac Over.java
Over.java:6: method does not override a method from its superclass
        @Override
        ^
1 error
```

Thus, you can fix the problem sooner and more cheaply because it is identified much earlier in the process.

JDK 6.0 Annotations

JSR 175 defined the original metadata facility of JDK 5.0. JSR 269 introduces the Pluggable Annotation Processing API, which is a part of JDK 6.0. This standardizes some processing that was difficult at best with JDK 5.0 when creating your own annotations. In addition to this standardization, JDK 6.0 adds its own set of new annotations, many of which have been described in earlier chapters. We'll look at the new annotations first.

New Annotations

There is no single place I could find that listed all the annotations, new and old. The best you can do is grep through the source and find the classes defined with an @interface, as in the following line:

```
public @interface ResultColumn {
```

When defining your own annotations, that is the syntax for how they are declared.

Here is information about all the annotations in JDK 6.0. Why use them for your classes? Because tools that know about them can be made smarter to make your life as a developer easier.

The java.beans Package

The first annotation, @ConstructorProperties, is used in conjunction with a JavaBeans component constructor. If you are using a third-party library with an IDE and don't necessarily know the names or order of the arguments to the constructor (but you do know their types), the @ConstructorProperties annotation can be used to designate their appropriate order by name. Thus, the IDE can present names for arguments, not just types. Listing 10-4 shows what using the @ConstructorProperties annotation might look like for a fictitious Point class with two properties, x and y, of the same type.

Listing 10-4. *@ConstructorProperties Annotation Usage*

```java
import java.beans.ConstructorProperties;

public class Point {
  private double x, y;

  public Point() {
  }

  @ConstructorProperties({"x", "y"})
  public Point(double x, double y) {
    this.x = x;
    this.y = y;
  }

  public double getX() {
    return x;
  }

  public double getY() {
    return y;
  }

  public void setX(double x) {
    this.x = x;
  }

  public void setY(double y) {
    this.y = y;
  }
}
```

By specifying the names x and y as arguments to @ConstructorProperties, you are saying that methods named getX() and getY() are available to access the property values. And, of course, that x comes first in the argument list.

■**Tip** As in Listing 10-4 with the import java.beans.ConstructorProperties; line, don't forget to import the classes for the annotations. Without the import line, the compiler will look in the default package for the annotation class (@ConstructorProperties here). The compiler has no internal mapping of annotations to classes in other packages.

At least for the early access releases of JDK 6.0, Sun has yet to add `@ConstructorProperties` lines to the core library classes that are typically used as JavaBeans components. So, if you use an IDE, the core classes won't act smart and show the extra information about parameter order for constructors.

The java.lang Package

No new annotations here. Just the original three: `@Deprecated`, `@Override`, and `@SuppressWarnings`.

The java.lang.annotation Package

This package is primarily for the library support for the annotation facility. It includes four annotations that help annotation creators document the proper usage of their annotations. These were part of JDK 5.0, and are not new to Mustang.

- `Documented`: States whether the annotation should be documented by javadoc.

- `Inherited`: States that a parent class should be queried when an annotation is not found in main class.

- `Retention`: Identifies how long the annotation is retained. The enumeration `RetentionPolicy` offers three possible settings: `SOURCE`, `CLASS`, and `RUNTIME`. A setting of `SOURCE` means that the annotation is only needed to compile; `CLASS` means that the data is stored in the class file, but isn't necessarily used by the virtual machine (VM); and `RUNTIME` means that the VM retains it and thus can be read if requested.

- `Target`: Identifies the program element associated with the metadata. The `ElementType` enumeration offers eight possible values: `ANNOTATION_TYPE`, `CONSTRUCTOR`, `FIELD`, `LOCAL_VARIABLE`, `METHOD`, `PACKAGE`, `PARAMETER`, and `TYPE`.

The java.sql Package

The four `java.sql` annotations were explored in Chapter 5: `@AutoGeneratedKeys`, `@ResultColumn`, `@Select`, and `@Update`. See Chapter 5 for more information on them.

The javax.annotation Package

Six annotations are found in the `javax.annotation` package. These are heavily weighted toward usage with the enterprise edition of the Java platform, but are a standard part of Java SE 6. When used, they can provide additional information to the application server.

- Generated: Used to flag autogenerated source. Usage would include the value of the source generator:

```
@Generated("net.zukowski.revealed.FooGenerator")
```

- InjectionComplete: Used to flag methods to be called after insertion into the container.

- PostConstruct: Used to flag initialization methods to be called after construction.

- PreDestroy: Used to flag methods that release resources upon finalization of class usage—such as when removed from an EJB container. For instance, if PostConstruct got a database connection, then PreDestroy would probably close it.

```
private DataSource aDB;
private Connection connection;

@Resource
private void setADB(DataSource ds) {
    aDB = ds;
}

@PostConstruct
private void initialize() {
    connection = aDB.getConnection();
}
@PreDestroy
private void cleanup() {
    connection.close();
}
```

- Resource: Used to declare a reference to a resource. The name specified would be the JNDI name of the resource. For instance, to look up the JNDI resource named fooDB, use the following:

```
@Resource(name="fooDB")
private DataSource aDB;
```

- Resources: Used to block multiple Resource declarations together.

```
@Resources ({
  @Resource(name="fooDB" type=javax.sql.DataSource),
  @Resource(name="fooMQ" type=javax.jms.ConnectionFactory)
})
```

■**Tip** If you declare your own annotations, keep in mind the pattern shown here. Repeated annotations are not allowed, so they must be grouped together into a single annotation.

The javax.annotation.processing Package

The annotations found in the `javax.annotation.processing` package are used by the capabilities added with JSR 269 for annotation processing. There are three annotations there: `SupportedAnnotationTypes`, `SupportedOptions`, and `SupportedSourceVersion`. Each of these will be described later in the chapter, in the "Annotation Processing" section.

The javax.management Package

The two annotations found in the `javax.management` package are `DescriptorKey` and `MXBean`. If you are familiar with the Java Management Extensions, their usage will prove helpful.

The `DescriptorKey` annotation is for describing annotation elements related to a field. For an attribute, operation, or construction, you can add descriptors such that when the resulting descriptor is created, you can configure its values. See the javadoc for the `DescriptorKey` annotation for more information about auto-conversion of annotation elements, such as rules for how a primitive becomes an object.

The `MXBean` annotation is used to explicitly tag an interface as an `MXBean` interface or not. If the interface name ends in `MXBean`, it is an `MXBean` interface by default. If it doesn't, then the interface isn't an `MXBean`-related interface. The `@MXBean` annotation allows you to tag an interface as an `MXBean` if it doesn't end with `MXBean`, and allows you to reject the automatic association if you don't want it.

For the positive case, the following three declarations in Listing 10-5 are defined to be `MXBean` interfaces, assuming proper imports.

Listing 10-5. *@MXBean Annotation Usage*

```
// Default naming
public interface MyMXBean {
}

@MXBean
public interface MyInterface1 {
}

@MXBean(true)
public interface MyInterface2 {
}
```

For the negative cases, there are only two:

```
// Default naming
public interface MyClass {
}

@MXBean(false)
public interface MyMXBean {
}
```

The javax.xml.bind.annotation Package

The `javax.xml.bind.annotation` package is for customizing Java program elements to an XML Schema mapping, as shown in Chapter 6. It defines the annotations shown in Table 10-1.

Table 10-1. *Annotations Found in the javax.xml.bind.annotation Package*

Annotation	Description
XmlAccessorOrder	Controls the ordering of fields and properties in a class
XmlAccessorType	Controls whether fields or JavaBean properties are serialized by default
XmlAnyAttribute	Maps a JavaBean property to a map of wildcard attributes
XmlAnyElement	Maps a JavaBean property to an XML infoset representation and/or JAXB element
XmlAttachmentRef	Marks a field/property to indicate that its XML form is a URI reference to mime content
XmlAttribute	Maps a JavaBean property to an XML attribute
XmlElement	Maps a JavaBean property to an XML element derived from the property name
XmlElementDecl	Maps a factory method to an XML element
XmlElementRef	Maps a JavaBean property to an XML element derived from the property's type
XmlElementRefs	Marks a property that refers to classes with XmlElement or JAXBElement
XmlElements	Contains multiple @XmlElement annotations
XmlElementWrapper	Generates a wrapper element around an XML representation
XmlEnum	Maps an enumeration of type Enum to an XML representation
XmlEnumValue	Maps an enumerated constant in an Enum type to XML representation
XmlID	Maps a JavaBean property to XML ID

Annotation	Description
XmlIDREF	Maps a JavaBean property to XML IDREF
XmlInlineBinaryData	Disables consideration of XOP encoding for data types that are bound to base64-encoded binary data in XML
XmlList	Maps a property to a list simple type
XmlMimeType	Associates the mime type that controls the XML representation of the property
XmlMixed	Annotates a JavaBean multivalued property to support mixed content
XmlNs	Associates a namespace prefix with an XML namespace URI
XmlRegistry	Marks a class that has XML element factories
XmlRootElement	Maps a class or an enumerated type to an XML element
XmlSchema	Maps a package name to an XML namespace
XmlSchemaType	Maps a Java type to a simple schema built-in type
XmlSchemaTypes	Contains multiple @XmlSchemaType annotations
XmlTransient	Prevents the mapping of a JavaBean property to an XML representation
XmlType	Maps a class or an Enum type to an XML Schema type
XmlValue	Enables mapping a class to an XML Schema complex type with a simpleContent type or an XML Schema simple type

The javax.xml.bind.annotation.adapters Package

The javax.xml.bind.annotation.adapters package is for allowing Java classes to be used with JAXB. Again, this was shown in Chapter 6. There are two annotations in this package:

- XmlJavaTypeAdapter

- XmlJavaTypeAdapters

The javax.xml.ws Package

There are nine annotations found in the javax.xml.ws package. They are as follows:

- BindingType

- RequestWrapper

- ResponseWrapper

- ServiceMode

- WebEndpoint

- WebFault

- WebServiceClient

- WebServiceProvider

- WebServiceRef

These annotations are part of the core Java API for XML Web Services (JAX-WS) APIs. These were also explored in Chapter 6.

Annotation Processing

Enough about what annotations are out there. Let's take a look at what you can do with them when writing them yourself. First, we'll take a quick look at the 5.0 way of annotation processing. Then we'll move on to the new way.

J2SE 5.0 Processing

The way to process annotations with J2SE 5.0 was to use a library called the Mirror API. The Mirror API contains two parts: one for the processor, in the `com.sun.mirror.apt` package; and the other for a series of support classes that model the language. The language modeling piece stays put for Java SE 6, while the `apt` pieces relocate to the `javax.annotation.processing` package, with a few changes.

■**Note** For information on the Mirror API, visit `http://java.sun.com/j2se/1.5.0/docs/guide/apt/mirror/overview-summary.html`. It is now released under a BSD license and available at `https://aptmirrorapi.dev.java.net`.

To learn about the language modeling piece, you'll write a short little processor that walks through the classes found in the classpath and generates a list of all methods of all classes found. This doesn't involve writing any new tags, just processing information already made available by the runtime environment. A slightly different form of this example is part of the documentation that comes with the `apt` tool.

To get started, you need to create an implementation of the `com.sun.mirror.apt.`
`AnnotationProcessorFactory` interface. There are three methods to the interface, as
follows:

- `AnnotationProcessor getProcessorFor(Set<AnnotationTypeDeclaration> atds,`
  `AnnotationProcessorEnvironment env)`

- `Collection<String> supportedAnnotationTypes()`

- `Collection<String> supportedOptions()`

Note For Java SE 6.0, the latter two methods here, `supportedAnnotationTypes()` and
`supportedOptions()`, have become annotations themselves.

The first method is what is used to "look up" the annotation processor. All the
method needs to do is return a new instance of your class, which implements
`AnnotationProcessor`.

The processor interface implementation is the worker bee. It has a single method to
implement: `process()`. If you use the `AnnotationProcessorEnvironment` implementation
passed into the constructor of your `AnnotationProcessor`, your `process()` method loops
through all the declarations requested.

The `AnnotationProcessorEnvironment` offers different ways to request declarations. The
`Collection<Declaration> getDeclarationsAnnotatedWith(AnnotationTypeDeclaration a)`
method allows you to ask for those declarations (methods, classes, and fields) defined
with a particular annotation. The `Collection<TypeDeclaration> getSpecifiedType➡`
`Declarations()` method essentially allows you to get all of them, giving you access to
everything passed from the command line. Lastly, `Collection<TypeDeclaration>`
`getTypeDeclarations()` doesn't require you to specify everything. For the sample in
Listing 10-6, use the `getSpecifiedTypeDeclarations()` variety.

To process each declaration, you need a "visitor." The `com.sun.mirror.util` package
offers the `DeclarationVisitor` interface and `SimpleDeclarationVisitor` implementation to
help. The `DeclarationVisitor` interface offers a series of `visitXXXDeclaration()` methods
so that you can choose to work with only certain types of declarations, such as all the
classes, all the interfaces, or all the methods. For instance, to print out the name of each
class, you would override the `visitClassDeclaration()` method.

```
public void visitClassDeclaration(ClassDeclaration d) {
  System.out.println(d.getQualifiedName());
}
```

Listing 10-6 puts all the pieces together to define an annotation processor that prints out the specified classes and interfaces, along with the names of their methods (though not the constructors, which requires another visit*XXX*Declaration() method implemented).

Listing 10-6. *J2SE 5.0 Annotation Processor*

```
import com.sun.mirror.apt.*;
import com.sun.mirror.declaration.*;
import com.sun.mirror.type.*;
import com.sun.mirror.util.*;
import static com.sun.mirror.util.DeclarationVisitors.*;

import java.util.*;


public class DumpFactory implements AnnotationProcessorFactory {
  // Process all annotations
  private static final Collection<String> supportedAnnotations
    = Collections.unmodifiableCollection(Arrays.asList("*"));

  // No options support
  private static final Collection<String> supportedOptions = Collections.emptySet();

  public Collection<String> supportedAnnotationTypes() {
    return supportedAnnotations;
  }

  public Collection<String> supportedOptions() {
    return supportedOptions;
  }

  public AnnotationProcessor getProcessorFor(Set<AnnotationTypeDeclaration> atds,
      AnnotationProcessorEnvironment env) {
    return new DumpProcessor(env);
  }

  private static class DumpProcessor implements AnnotationProcessor {

    private final AnnotationProcessorEnvironment env;
```

```java
  DumpProcessor(AnnotationProcessorEnvironment env) {
    this.env = env;
  }

  public void process() {
    for (TypeDeclaration typeDecl : env.getSpecifiedTypeDeclarations()) {
      typeDecl.accept(getDeclarationScanner(new DumpVisitor(), NO_OP));
    }
  }

  private static class DumpVisitor extends SimpleDeclarationVisitor {
    public void visitMethodDeclaration(MethodDeclaration d) {
      System.out.println("\t" + d.getSimpleName());
    }
    public void visitClassDeclaration(ClassDeclaration d) {
      System.out.println(d.getQualifiedName());
    }
    public void visitInterfaceDeclaration(InterfaceDeclaration d) {
      System.out.println(d.getQualifiedName());
    }
  }
 }
}
```

Defining the class is the easy part. Compiling it is just step one, and you can't just use javac alone (yet). As previously mentioned, you need to include tools.jar in your class-path to compile an annotation.

```
javac -cp c:\jdk1.6.0\lib\tools.jar DumpFactory.java
```

■Note At least for now, you have to manually include tools.jar in your classpath to compile annotation processors. It is possible that by the time Java SE 6 ships, that could change.

Running of the annotation is not done with the java command. This is where apt comes into play. But before you can use apt, you have to package up the factory and processor into a JAR file and "install" it, like other items that use the service API. Typically, this is done by creating a file in META-INF/services named com.sun.mirror.apt. AnnotationProcessorFactory to point to the processor just defined. However, to avoid this step, you can include extra command-line options to the apt command. And, for a little test, just run the processor on itself.

```
> apt -cp c:\jdk1.6.0\lib\tools.jar;. -factory DumpFactory DumpFactory.java
DumpFactory
        supportedAnnotationTypes
        supportedOptions
        getProcessorFor
DumpFactory.DumpProcessor
        process
DumpFactory.DumpProcessor.DumpVisitor
        visitMethodDeclaration
        visitClassDeclaration
        visitInterfaceDeclaration
```

Those are the basics of processing annotations with JDK 5.0.

Java SE 6.0 Processing

Moving to the Java SE 6.0 world changes a few things. The primary difference is the moving of the annotation processing library into a more standard javax package and doing away with the factory. Secondly, the javac command-line tool now offers a -processor option to run a previously created processor.

The removal of the factory is actually an interesting twist and makes total sense. All the factory did was return a single processor. So now the AbstractProcessor class forms the basis of all processors and really just is the processor—unlike with 5.0, in which you had to create an extra class. Ignoring the imports and a few other things, your basic processor definition is shown here:

```
public class Dump6Processor extends AbstractProcessor {

  public boolean process(Set<? extends TypeElement> annotations,
      RoundEnvironment roundEnv) {

    return false; // No annotations claimed
  }
}
```

To demonstrate, Listing 10-7 creates a processor that lists the annotations in the classes specified. This is where new the annotations of the javax.annotation.processing package are used: SupportedSourceVersion, SupportedAnnotationTypes, and SupportedOptions. The source version is specified by one of the constants of the SourceVersion enumeration of the java.lang.model package. The SupportedAnnotationTypes annotation is just like the supportedAnnotationTypes() method of the JDK 5.0 processor factory, and the SupportedOptions annotation mirrors supportedOptions(). When not specified, it defaults to returning an empty set.

Beyond the annotations, all the processor does is loop through each annotation and print its name and nesting kind (level of declaration). More typically, if the annotation was something to be processed, you would use the accept() method on the TypeElement and "visit" it.

Listing 10-7. *Java SE 6.0 Annotation Processor*

```java
import javax.annotation.processing.*;
import javax.lang.model.*;
import javax.lang.model.element.*;

import java.util.*;

// Source version
@SupportedSourceVersion(SourceVersion.RELEASE_6)

// Process all annotations
@SupportedAnnotationTypes("*")

// No options support
// Empty set when not annotated with @SupportedOptions

public class Dump6Processor extends AbstractProcessor {

  public boolean process(Set<? extends TypeElement> annotations,
      RoundEnvironment roundEnv) {

    if (!roundEnv.processingOver()) {
      for (TypeElement element : annotations) {
        System.out.println(element.getQualifiedName() +
          "(" + element.getNestingKind() + ")");
      }
    }
    return false; // No annotations claimed
  }
}
```

Again, compilation requires the tools.jar file, as follows:

```
javac -cp c:\jdk1.6.0\lib\tools.jar Dump6Processor.java
```

Now compile this with the -processor option to javac:

```
> javac -processor Dump6Processor Dump6Processor.java
javax.annotation.processing.SupportedSourceVersion(TOP_LEVEL)
javax.annotation.processing.SupportedAnnotationTypes(TOP_LEVEL)
warning: No annotation processors claimed present annotation types:
  [javax.annotation.processing.SupportedSourceVersion,
  javax.annotation.processing.SupportedAnnotationTypes]
```

Note The javac command-line tool is getting "more" like java in Java SE 6.0 through the addition of command-line options. In fact, some are even nonstandard. Try out the -Xprint option with javac to get information similar to what you get from javap and -XprintRounds or -XprintProcessorInfo to monitor processing tasks. Options like -Xmaxerrs and -Xmaxwarns (which limit the maximum number of errors and warnings, respectively) are not new to Java SE 6.0.

The processingOver() check in process() is necessary, as a processor could be called multiple times in one javac execution. More typically, a processor would actually do something with the annotation, such as generate a file. As far as generating the file, the old AnnotationProcessorEnvironment interface of the com.sun.mirror.apt package is now the new ProcessingEnvironment interface of the javax.annotation.processing package. In both cases, you get a Filer to hold the generated output.

```
Writer out = env.getFiler().createTextFile(
    Filer.Location.SOURCE_TREE, package, path, charset)
```

Summary

Most people aren't going to create their own annotation processors. They're more apt to use annotations created by others, like for JDBC queries. If you only use them, you don't need to know anything in this chapter. If you need to process annotations, however, you need to know how the processing model has changed from J2SE 5.0 to Java SE 6.0. It's not that different—just slightly—with classes moving between packages and slightly different interfaces. Use them with care, and don't go overboard. Defining your own annotations really has not changed from J2SE 5.0.

Appendix A wraps up the book with information about acquiring the weekly releases.

Licensing, Installation, and Participation

Just when is the right time to release software to the masses? With Mustang, the masses have had access since February 2005. With roughly weekly releases since then, one was able to monitor the progress of both the API development and the completion of the new feature sets for what would become known as Java SE 6.

■Note The information in this chapter is valid as of spring 2006. When Mustang moved into beta release, locations didn't move, but they are apt to move later, and it is unknown how much information will be left behind on the original java.net site after Java SE 6 is released.

Snapshot Releases

The home for early Mustang access has been the java.net portal. Powered by CollabNet and co-run by Sun and O'Reilly, developers can visit `https://mustang.dev.java.net` and download the latest early access release of Mustang. With a separate download, you can also download the javadoc for the core classes. And, if you agree to the necessary licensing terms, you can also download the complete source snapshots for all of Mustang—not just the `java` and `javax` packages, but the `sun` packages, too. With the last download, instructions are provided to compile the full system and build everything yourself.

Licensing Terms

First off, let me state that I am not a lawyer, and what I say cannot be construed as legal advice; this is just my understanding of Sun's licensing terms. As far as licensing goes,

Sun has been reluctant to release the core Java release as open source. While Apache Harmony (`http://incubator.apache.org/harmony`) incubates along as an open source J2SE 5.0 implementation, you can't get the source for the core system of Mustang unless you're in an unrestricted country and you agree to the Java Research License (JRL). Iran, North Korea, and Cuba: no. United States, Canada, France, and England: yes. (That is not a complete list in either case.) It appears that Sun doesn't require you to follow their Sun Community Source License (SCSL) for research related to java.net projects.

The SCSL is Sun's attempt to open up source somewhat, but not totally. It is geared toward the commercial community and allows that community to offer proprietary modifications and extensions to a particular area, while maintaining compatibility through technology compatibility kits (TCKs). You can get a more complete overview of the license at `www.sun.com/software/communitysource/overview.xml`.

On the other hand, the JRL is geared more toward internal non-production research and development uses. If or when the project turns into something that is distributed, either internally or externally, you then must sign something called the Java Distribution License, which requires its own level of compatibility requirements. While the SCSL does offer a research section, the JRL is geared more toward the research community and universities. For more information on it, see `www.java.net/jrl.csp`.

Getting the Software

While JSR 270 describes Mustang (see `http://jcp.org/en/jsr/detail?id=270`), access to the software comes from the previously mentioned snapshot area. Starting at `https://mustang.dev.java.net` and following the "Latest Mustang binary snapshots" link takes you to the weekly binary snapshot drops. You'll find versions for the Microsoft Windows platform, Windows AMD64, Solaris SPARC, Solaris x86, Solaris AMD64, Linux, and Linux AMD64. Macintosh users will need to wait for Apple to release a version.

It is best to get the complete self-extracting JDK file for your platform; though if you're only interested in the Java Runtime Environment (JRE), it's available as a JAR file (a self-extracting DEBUG JAR file is also available).

Downloading and running the file displays a splash screen (see Figure A-1). Then you get to agree to the prerelease software evaluation agreement (shown in Figure A-2).

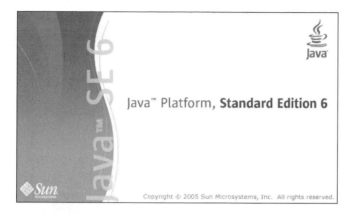

Figure A-1. *The splash screen for Mustang installation*

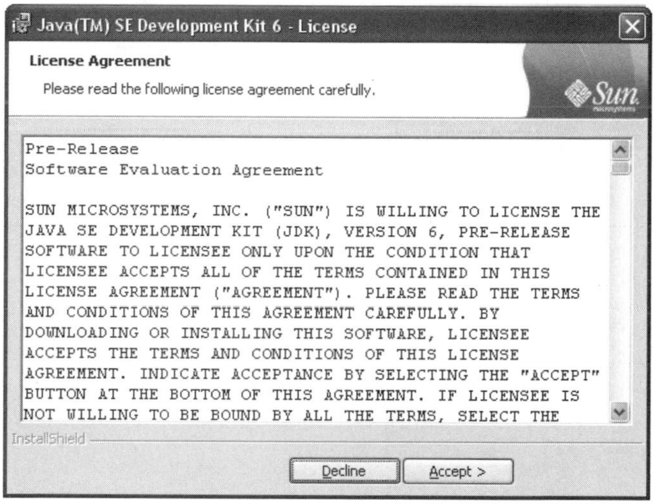

Figure A-2. *The license agreement*

After accepting the terms of the agreement, you'll see the Custom Setup screen (shown in Figure A-3). By default, everything gets installed into C:\Program Files\Java\ jdk1.6.0 (on a Windows platform). You can change this directory or choose not to install the demos, source code, or public JRE. You must install the development tools. Clicking Next starts the installation, after which you can monitor the progress (as shown in Figure A-4).

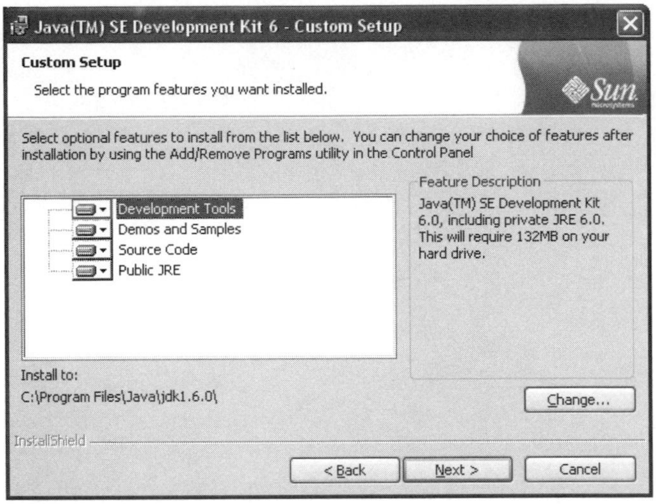

Figure A-3. *The Custom Setup screen for Mustang installation*

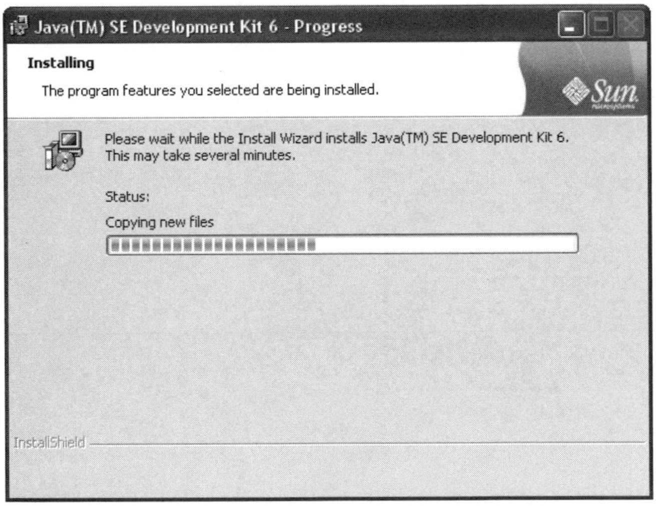

Figure A-4. *Installation progress status*

■**Note** Installation of the public JRE will display even more screenshots and an additional license that requires acceptance.

Once everything is done, you'll see a screen telling you that the installation is complete (shown in Figure A-5). You can then choose whether to see the README file or not. If you do, the README file is then displayed in a browser window. It has taken some time, but it now finally shows something relevant to Java 6. For the longest time, only Java 5 information was shown in the README. As is expected for prerelease software, some of the links sometimes didn't work (for example, the link to the installation instructions). I guess the links point to where things will be when Mustang is released—the joys of prerelease software.

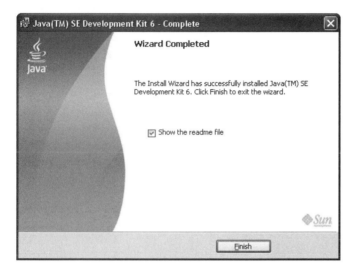

Figure A-5. *Installation complete*

In addition to getting the JDK, it is best to also get the javadocs. These come down in an installable JAR file. On the Binary Snapshot Releases web page (`http://download.java.net/jdk6/binaries`), just follow the first link on the second line, which reads "Java Docs (*XX* MB JAR / HTML)" (*XX* stands for the size of the JAR file).

Downloading and unzipping/unjarring the documentation is surprisingly not what you do. Instead, after downloading the file, you run it with the `java -jar jarfilename` command, replacing `jarfilename` with the name of the downloaded JAR file. This requires you to accept another license agreement (shown in Figure A-6) before choosing an installation directory. Personally, I tend to enter the same directory as the JDK installation. The documentation will then go into a `docs` subdirectory. Once installed, you should then bookmark the top-level javadoc page. Installation takes some time.

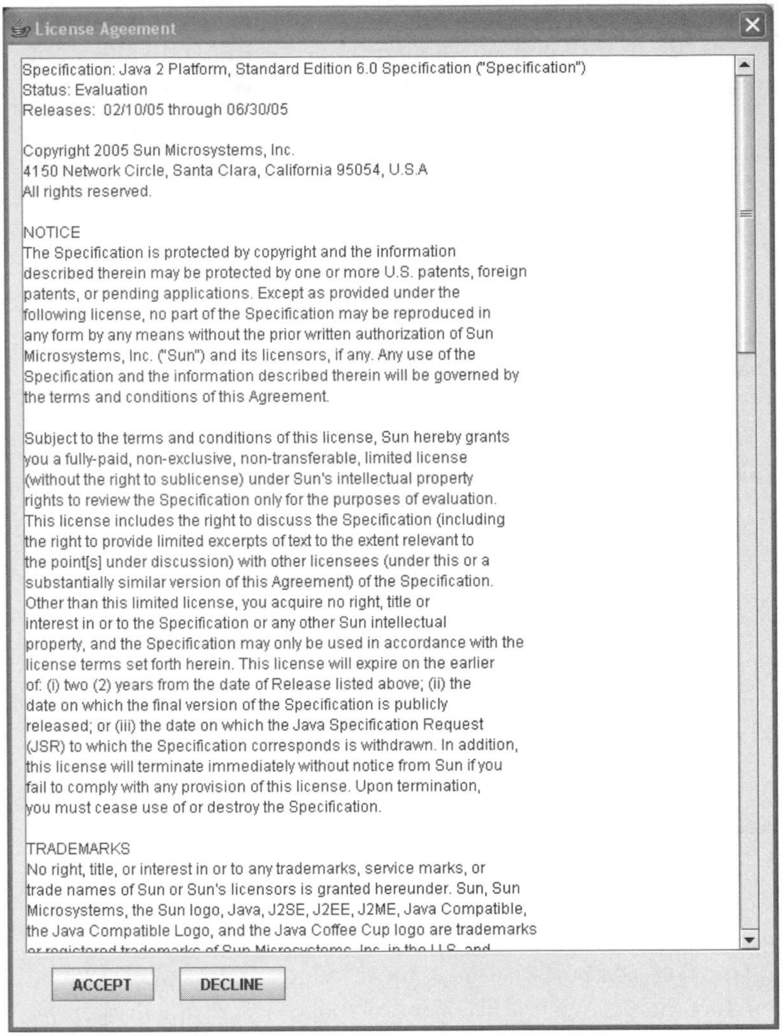

Figure A-6. *The documentation license agreement*

Caution When I installed the javadoc, the "install complete" window would hide in the background and not come to the foreground. I had to hunt it out to click OK to end the installation process.

Participation

The top-level Mustang page on `www.java.net` has a "How to contribute" link. Sun encourages developers to contribute to the code base for the Java platform and add to the robustness and stability of the release. While you can always log bugs or feature requests at `http://bugs.sun.com`, a more proactive approach has you actually submitting fixes to the problems. I have heard of developers who submitted fixes for problems lingering around for some time, but with no urgency to be fixed. You, too, can identify a problem and fix it. Of course, the job is unpaid and you are contributing to the success of a commercial product, not an open source effort. If it isn't too late in the release cycle and you choose to help, here are the steps you need to follow.

After agreeing to the JRL and downloading the source code, you need to apply for the role of `jdk.researcher`. You apply on the Project Membership/Role Request page at `http://jdk.dev.java.net/servlets/ProjectMembershipRequest`. If you are not yet a java.net member, you need to apply for membership there first. Terms of the `jdk.researcher` role are described on the Joining This Project page (`https://jdk.dev.java.net/terms.html`). The terms include acceptance of the JRL and the java.net web site Terms of Participation (`http://java.net/terms.csp`).

After your project role request is approved (which supposedly happens within one business day), you can go to the JDK-Collaboration Project page (`http://jdk-collaboration.dev.java.net`). You can't see the project information until your role request is approved.

Next, you need to print, read, and sign the Sun Contributor Agreement, and fax it to (650) 482-6557. The agreement itself can be found at `https://jdk.dev.java.net/Sun_Contributor_Agreement.pdf`. It provides Sun with the rights it needs to distribute your contributions to others. You can also scan the document and e-mail a signed agreement to `jdk-contributions@sun.com`. (Sun asks that you please write clearly.)

After you're accepted into the role of `jdk.researcher`, and Sun receives the fax, your project role becomes `jdk.contributor`. You are now able to submit your contributions.

When you contribute an enhancement or bug fix, you need to provide the necessary data for a senior Sun engineer to review and validate the correctness of the submission. You should also include a unit test that verifies the existence of the problem before the fix, and also verifies that the bug fix indeed fixes the problem. Some example contributions for bug fixes are shown at `https://mustang.dev.java.net/example-contribution.html`. Don't forget to include the bug number or incident number with the correction. If you don't have a bug number or incident number, submit a bug report first.

For additional information on the different roles in a java.net project, see the JDK Community Governance Guidelines (`https://jdk.dev.java.net/governance.html`).

When getting started, a good place to get answers to questions about Mustang is in Sun's forums, at `http://forums.java.net/jive/forum.jspa?forumID=23`.

Index

You Need the Companion eBook

Your purchase of this book entitles you to buy the companion PDF-version eBook for only $10. Take the weightless companion with you anywhere.

We believe this Apress title will prove so indispensable that you'll want to carry it with you everywhere, which is why we are offering the companion eBook (in PDF format) for $10 to customers who purchase this book now. Convenient and fully searchable, the PDF version of any content-rich, page-heavy Apress book makes a valuable addition to your programming library. You can easily find and copy code — or perform examples by quickly toggling between instructions and the application. Even simultaneously tackling a donut, diet soda, and complex code becomes simplified with hands-free eBooks!

Once you purchase your book, getting the $10 companion eBook is simple:

❶ Visit **www.apress.com/promo/tendollars/**.

❷ Complete a basic registration form to receive a randomly generated question about this title.

❸ Answer the question correctly in 60 seconds, and you will receive a promotional code to redeem for the $10.00 eBook.

2560 Ninth Street • Suite 219 • Berkeley, CA 94710

eBookshop   ASP Today   **Apress®**
THE EXPERT'S VOICE™

Offer valid through 1/24/07.